ClearRevise®

AQA GCSE
English Literature

Illustrated revision and practice

Romeo and Juliet
By William Shakespeare

Published by
PG Online Limited
The Old Coach House
35 Main Road
Tolpuddle
Dorset
DT2 7EW
United Kingdom

sales@pgonline.co.uk
www.clearrevise.com
www.pgonline.co.uk
2023

PREFACE

Absolute clarity! That's the aim.

This is everything you need to ace the question on *Romeo and Juliet* and beam with pride. The content is laid out in a beautifully illustrated format that is clear, approachable and as concise and simple as possible.

The checklist on the contents pages will help you keep track of what you have already worked through and what's left before the big day.

We have included worked exam-style questions with answers. There is also an exam-style question at the end of the book. You can check your answer against that given on page 60.

LEVELS OF LEARNING

Based on the degree to which you are able to truly understand a new topic, we recommend that you work in stages. Start by reading a short explanation of something, then try to recall what you've just read. This will have a limited effect if you stop there but it aids the next stage. Question everything. Write down your own summary and then complete and mark a related exam-style question. Cover up the answers if necessary but learn from them once you've seen them. Lastly, teach someone else. Explain the topic in a way that they can understand. Have a go at the different practice questions – they offer an insight into how and where marks are awarded.

Design and artwork: Jessica Webb / PG Online Ltd

First edition 2023 10 9 8 7 6 5 4 3 2 1
A catalogue entry for this book is available from the British Library
ISBN: 978-1-910523-93-3
Copyright © PG Online 2023
All rights reserved
No part of this publication may be reproduced, stored in a retrieval system, or transmitted in any form or by any means without the prior written permission of the copyright owner.

Printed on FSC® certified paper by Bell and Bain Ltd, Glasgow, UK.

THE SCIENCE OF REVISION

Illustrations and words

Research has shown that revising with words and pictures doubles the quality of responses by students.[1] This is known as 'dual-coding' because it provides two ways of fetching the information from our brain. The improvement in responses is particularly apparent in students when they are asked to apply their knowledge to different problems. Recall, application and judgement are all specifically and carefully assessed in public examination questions.

Retrieval of information

Retrieval practice encourages students to come up with answers to questions.[2] The closer the question is to one you might see in a real examination, the better. Also, the closer the environment in which a student revises is to the 'examination environment', the better. Students who had a test 2–7 days away did 30% better using retrieval practice than students who simply read, or repeatedly reread material. Students who were expected to teach the content to someone else after their revision period did better still.[3] What was found to be most interesting in other studies is that students using retrieval methods and testing for revision were also more resilient to the introduction of stress.[4]

Ebbinghaus' forgetting curve and spaced learning

Ebbinghaus' 140-year-old study examined the rate at which we forget things over time. The findings still hold true. However, the act of forgetting facts and techniques and relearning them is what cements them into the brain.[5] Spacing out revision is more effective than cramming – we know that, but students should also know that the space between revisiting material should vary depending on how far away the examination is. A cyclical approach is required. An examination 12 months away necessitates revisiting covered material about once a month. A test in 30 days should have topics revisited every 3 days – intervals of roughly a tenth of the time available.[6]

Summary

Students: the more tests and past questions you do, in an environment as close to examination conditions as possible, the better you are likely to perform on the day. If you prefer to listen to music while you revise, tunes without lyrics will be far less detrimental to your memory and retention. Silence is most effective.[5] If you choose to study with friends, choose carefully – effort is contagious.[7]

---

1. Mayer, R. E., & Anderson, R. B. (1991). Animations need narrations: An experimental test of dual-coding hypothesis. *Journal of Education Psychology*, (83)4, 484–490.
2. Roediger III, H. L., & Karpicke, J.D. (2006). Test-enhanced learning: Taking memory tests improves long-term retention. *Psychological Science*, 17(3), 249–255.
3. Nestojko, J., Bui, D., Kornell, N. & Bjork, E. (2014). Expecting to teach enhances learning and organisation of knowledge in free recall of text passages. *Memory and Cognition*, 42(7), 1038–1048.
4. Smith, A. M., Floerke, V. A., & Thomas, A. K. (2016) Retrieval practice protects memory against acute stress. *Science*, 354(6315), 1046–1048.
5. Perham, N., & Currie, H. (2014). Does listening to preferred music improve comprehension performance? *Applied Cognitive Psychology*, 28(2), 279–284.
6. Cepeda, N. J., Vul, E., Rohrer, D., Wixted, J. T. & Pashler, H. (2008). Spacing effects in learning a temporal ridgeline of optimal retention. *Psychological Science*, 19(11), 1095–1102.
7. Busch, B. & Watson, E. (2019), *The Science of Learning*, 1st ed. Routledge.

CONTENTS

Assessment objectives vi

Context, language and structure

Shakespeare and *Romeo and Juliet* 2
Context 3
Features of plays 6
Shakespeare's language 7
Language techniques 10

Analysis of acts

Act 1, Prologue & Scene 1 12
Act 1, Scenes 1–2 13
Act 1, Scene 3 14
Act 1, Scenes 4–5 15
Act 2, Prologue & Scenes 1–2 16
Act 2, Scenes 2–3 17
Act 2, Scenes 3–4 18
Act 2, Scenes 4–6 19
Act 3, Scene 1 20
Act 3, Scenes 1–2 21
Act 3, Scenes 2–3 22
Act 3, Scenes 4–5 23
Act 3, Scene 5 24
Act 4, Scene 1 25
Act 4, Scenes 2–3 26
Act 4, Scenes 4–5 27
Act 5, Scene 1 28
Act 5, Scenes 2–3 29
Act 5, Scene 3 30

Analysis of characters

Characters: Romeo Montague	31	☐
Characters: Juliet Capulet	36	☐
Characters: Friar Lawrence	41	☐
Characters: Mercutio	42	☐
Characters: The Nurse	43	☐
Characters: Tybalt and Paris	44	☐
Characters: Benvolio and the Prince	45	☐
Characters: The Capulets	46	☐
Characters: The Montagues	47	☐

Analysis of themes

Themes: Love	48	☐
Themes: Fate and free will	52	☐
Themes: Conflict	54	☐
Themes: Gender	58	☐

Examination practice **59**
Examination practice answers 60
Levels-based mark schemes for extended response questions 61
Index 62
Acknowledgments 64
Examination tips **65**

MARK ALLOCATIONS

All the questions in this book require extended responses. These answers should be marked as a whole in accordance with the levels of response guidance on **page 61**. The answers provided are examples only. There are many more points to make than there are marks available, so the answers are not exhaustive.

ASSESSMENT OBJECTIVES

In the exam, your answers will be marked against assessment objectives (AOs). It's important you understand which skills each AO tests.

AO1
- Show the ability to read, understand and respond to texts.
- Answers should maintain a critical style and develop an informed personal response.
- Use examples from the text, including quotes, to support and illustrate points.

AO2
- Analyse the language, form and structure used by a writer to create meanings and effects, using relevant subject terminology where appropriate.

AO3
- Show understanding of the relationships between texts and the contexts in which they were written.

AO4
- Use a range of vocabulary and sentence structures for clarity, purpose and effect, with accurate spelling and punctuation.

The AOs on this page have been written in simple language. See the AQA website for the official wording.

PAPER 1
Shakespeare and the 19th-century novel

Information about Paper 1

Written exam: 1 hour 45 minutes (this includes the question on the 19th-century novel)

64 marks (30 marks for Shakespeare plus 4 marks for SPaG, and 30 marks for 19th-century novel)

40% of the qualification grade (20% each for Shakespeare and the 19th-century novel)

Questions
One extended-writing question per text

SHAKESPEARE AND *ROMEO AND JULIET*

Romeo and Juliet is a play by William Shakespeare. It was written between 1594–1596.

William Shakespeare

William Shakespeare (1564–1616) is one of the best-known English authors. He's most famous for his plays (he wrote at least 37 in his lifetime), but he also wrote poetry.

Romeo and Juliet includes several **sonnets** (a form of poetry). See **page 9** for more on sonnets.

Shakespeare's plays can be broadly grouped into: **comedies** (humorous plays), **histories** (plays about historical figures) and **tragedies** (plays with unhappy endings). *Romeo and Juliet* is one of his most famous tragedies.

William Shakespeare

Although it's a tragedy, *Romeo and Juliet* also has some romantic and funny bits. These light-hearted moments prevent the play from being overwhelmingly sad.

Tragedies

Tragedies have been written since the time of Ancient Greece, and they usually have the following features:

1

A **protagonist** (main character) who is of high social standing (e.g. a king or noble).

Romeo is the son of Lord and Lady Montague. Juliet is the daughter of Lord and Lady Capulet. Both the Montague and Capulet families are wealthy nobles.

2

The protagonist has a **fatal flaw** (a characteristic which contributes to their downfall).

Both Romeo and Juliet's fatal flaw is their tendency to behave impulsively. This trait ultimately leads to their double suicide.

3

An **antagonist** (the protagonist's rival) who helps bring about the demise of the protagonist.

The rivalry between the Montague family and the Capulet family prevents Romeo and Juliet from being together and contributes to their deaths.

Tragedies are supposed to provoke **catharsis** from the audience. Catharsis describes a purging of emotions through art.

CONTEXT

Romeo and Juliet was written for 16th-century audiences. The context of the 1500s is important for understanding the deeper meaning of the play.

 You need to comment on the play's context to get marks for AO3 (see **page vi**).

Context

Background

Shakespeare based his play on pre-existing versions of the story of *Romeo and Juliet*, including *The Tragicall Historye of Romeus and Juliet* which was a narrative poem by Arthur Brooke published in 1562. Brooke's version was translated from an earlier Italian story.

Setting

Romeo and Juliet is set in the Italian city of Verona. It's never revealed exactly when the play takes place, but it's thought to be in the 14th or 15th century.

Italy would have seemed very exotic and exciting to Elizabethan audiences. Sixteenth-century audiences also believed that warm weather encouraged intense behaviour, so audiences would have expected the characters to behave passionately.

Comment: Setting the play in Italy meant that Shakespeare could criticise society or explore controversial topics without offending the English monarch, Queen Elizabeth I.

Offending the monarch could be considered an act of treason, which was punishable by death.

Other than setting the play in Italy and using some Italian-sounding names, the characters in the play speak English and have English attitudes and values.

Gender roles

In the 16th-century, gender roles were fixed. Society was **patriarchal**: men were the head of the household, and wives and daughters were supposed to be subservient to their fathers and husbands. It was a woman's duty to marry young and have lots of children.

Comment: Lady Capulet was already married with a child by the time she was 13. This was normal for society at the time.

Arranged marriages were common, especially between noblemen and noblewomen. Marriages were an opportunity for families to gain wealth, power or status, and the couple's feelings towards each other weren't really considered.

Comment: In Act 1, Scene 3, Lady Capulet encourages Juliet to marry Paris, even though the couple have never met.

Men were expected to provide for their families and protect their households from violence and dishonour.

Comment: When Romeo gate-crashes the Capulets' party, Tybalt sees it as his duty to fight Romeo to defend his family's honour.

For more on the theme of gender, turn to **page 58**.

GCSE English Literature | Romeo and Juliet

Context continued

Religion

Religion was a very important part of society in the 16th century, and everyone was expected to believe in God, go to hurch and live a moral life that avoided sin. People who didn't believe in God or didn't repent their sins were thought to spend eternity in hell.

Friar Lawrence represents religion. Romeo and Juliet go to him for advice.

During the 16th century, England's official religion switched from Catholicism to Protestantism. Being a Catholic in England in the late 1500s could lead to severe punishment.

Italy was (and still is) a predominately Catholic country, so the characters in the play are Catholic.

Juliet pretends to go to confession in Act 2, Scene 6 and Act 4, Scene 1. Confession is a Catholic practice where someone admits to sinful behaviour and asks a member of clergy for forgiveness.

Unlike today, couples could only get married in a church because weddings were a religious ceremony conducted before God. Women were expected to be virgins before they married, and having sex outside of marriage was taboo.

Comment: Juliet is a virgin before marriage, and the couple only have sex after their wedding.

Couples were expected to have sex very soon after getting married to 'consummate' the marriage (make the union official). Once a marriage had been consummated, it was almost impossible for the couple to end their marriage. Divorce was not an option.

Comment: Marriages which weren't consummated could be annulled. This means that when Romeo and Juliet sleep together, their marriage is formalised.

Bigamy (being married to more than one person) was a sin.

Comment: Juliet is prepared to fake her own death, rather than marry Paris. She knows that marrying Paris while she's still married to Romeo would be a sin, as she would be breaking her vows to both Romeo and God.

Suicide was also seen as a sin. The Church taught that only God should be able to determine when a person should die.

Comment: Although Romeo and Juliet try to avoid sinful behaviour throughout the play (such as getting married before having sex, and avoiding bigamy), they ultimately commit a sin by taking their own lives. This suggests that they would rather face the consequences of their sinful behaviour in hell than live without one another, reinforcing the strength of their love.

The theatre

In the 16th century, going to the theatre was very popular with both rich and poor people. There was a lot of demand for new plays, and Shakespeare's plays had to appeal to all members of society. He included rude humour to appeal to poorer audience members, as well as more refined language that would have appealed to the wealthier (and more educated) audience members.

Comment: Mercutio and the Nurse often use crude humour to decrease the tension and provide comic relief for the audience.

Inside a replica Shakespearian theatre.

Richer members of the audience could afford to sit in covered balconies, whereas poorer audience members would have stood in front of the stage in an area known as the pit, which was open to the elements.

Female roles were played by men, usually young boys, because it was illegal for women to perform onstage.

Comment: Juliet, the Nurse and Ladies Montague and Capulet would have all been played by men and boys originally.

Elizabethan plays didn't use detailed sets, so Shakespeare often used dialogue to clarify where the action was taking place or what the characters can see.

Chorus	*In fair Verona where we lay our scene.*	The audience are told in the Prologue where the action takes place.
Benvolio	*He ran this way and leapt this orchard wall.*	Benvolio explains how Romeo is able to run away from them after the Capulets' party.
Romeo	*And in his needy shop a tortoise hung,* *An alligator stuffed, and other skins*	Romeo describes the apothecary's shop in Act 5, Scene 1 to help the audience imagine what it looks like.

GCSE **English Literature** | Romeo and Juliet

FEATURES OF PLAYS

Plays are written to be performed, rather than read, so there are features in a playscript which are different to novels.

Acts and scenes

There are five **acts** in *Romeo and Juliet*, and each act is broken down into **scenes**. A new scene starts when the setting changes location.

The lines in the script are usually numbered. Numbering restarts with each new scene. Numbering helps to navigate the script easily.

Stage directions

Stage directions are used to tell a director how the play should be performed and to guide the actors. Some stage directions tell actors when to enter or exit the stage or how to deliver a line, whereas some stage directions help to create a certain atmosphere or create tension, for example, information about settings or sound effects.

Enter LADY CAPULET and NURSE

Exeunt — This means that more than one actor should leave the stage.

Aside — This means that the actor should say or do something away from the other characters.

Stage directions aren't supposed to be spoken.

When a character says their lines *aside*, this can be used to reveal a character's true feelings about something or to show that a character is behaving in a secretive way. It can also help to create **dramatic irony** (see page 11).

Music plays and they dance

Enter CAPULET in his gown

Enter FRIAR LAWRENCE, with a basket

A replica of Shakespeare's Globe Theatre in London.

Most of Shakespeare's stage directions are brief. This is probably because Shakespeare would have directed his own plays, so knew exactly how he wanted them to be staged.

SHAKESPEARE'S LANGUAGE

Shakespeare's plays were written over 400 years ago, so the language and punctuation can be tricky for modern-day audiences to understand.

Pronouns

In the 16th century, people used second-person pronouns that are no longer used today:

> **thou / thee** – you
> **thy** – your
> **thine** – yours

The pronoun 'you' is sometimes spelt 'ye'.

Verbs

Some verbs are written with '-(s)t' at the end, for example 'didst', 'hadst', 'art'. These verbs agreed with the second person pronouns 'thou' and 'thee'. If you remove the 'st', the verb should be recognisable.

Thou didst	You did
Thee hadst	You had
Thou art	You are

Some verbs are written with '-th' at the end. For example, 'hath' and 'doth'. These verbs agree with third person pronouns, e.g. 'he', 'she' and 'it'. If you remove the '-th', you should be able to recognise the verb.

He hath	He has
It doth	It does

Apostrophes

Sometimes letters have been removed from words and replaced with apostrophes. This can be done to adjust the number of syllables in the line and maintain the rhythm of the text.

> But saying o'er what I have said before:

> But saying **over** what I have said before:

For more information about the text's rhythm, turn to **page 8**.

 You need to comment on Shakespeare's language and dramatic techniques to get marks for AO2 (see **page vi**)

GCSE **English Literature** | Romeo and Juliet

Sentence order

The order that words appear in a sentence can sometimes seem unfamiliar. This is partly because word order was less fixed during Shakespeare's time, so words could be reordered to suit the rhythm of the lines.

Saw you him today? – Have you seen him today?

Rhythm and speech patterns

Verse

Most of the characters in *Romeo and Juliet* speak in **blank verse**. This means their lines don't rhyme, but they have a set rhythm, usually iambic pentameter.

Iambic pentameter

The majority of *Romeo and Juliet* is written in **iambic pentameter**. This is a specific rhythm where each line has ten syllables which alternate between unstressed and stressed syllables.

But **soft**, what **light** through **yon**der **win**dow **breaks**?

Shared lines

Occasionally, characters might split a line of iambic verse. This can show a close relationship between characters.

For example, in Act 1, Scene 4, Romeo and Mercutio share lines as they discuss going to the Capulets' party.

Romeo:	And we mean well in going to this mask, But 'tis no wit to go.
Mercutio:	Why, may one ask?

Shared lines show the closeness between Romeo and Mercutio.

Rhythm and speech patterns continued

Rhyming couplets

Rhyming couplets are two lines written in iambic pentameter which rhyme. They are sometimes used for emphasis at the end of a **soliloquy** (see page 10) or **monologue** (an extended speech by one person) or the closing lines of a scene.

| Benvolio | *And, as he fell, did Romeo turn and fly, This is the truth, or let Benvolio die.* | These lines end Benvolio's monologue in Act 3, Scene 1. |

| Romeo | *Hence will I to my ghostly sire's cell, His help to crave, and my dear hap to tell.* | These are the closing lines of Act 2, Scene 2. |

Sonnets

Sonnets are a type of poem. They have 14 lines, and are written in rhyming iambic pentameter.

Sonnets are associated with love poetry, so it's fitting that the lines that Romeo and Juliet share when they first meet in Act 1, Scene 5 take the form of a sonnet. The couple also complete each other's rhymes, showing their immediate connection.

> The Prologues in Act 1 and 2 are also sonnets.

Prose

Prose describes speech without a set rhythm. Prose can be used to show that a character is of a lower social class, for example Peter (the Capulets' servant), speaks in prose in Act 1, Scene 2.

| Peter | *Find them out whose names are written here! It is written that the shoemaker should meddle with his yard and the tailor with his last, the fisher with his pencil and the painter with his nets.* |

Mercutio, Benvolio and Romeo sometimes speak in prose when they are together. Prose makes their dialogue seem more relaxed and emphasises their informal relationship.

| Mercutio | *Come, come, thou art as hot a jack in thy mood as any in Italy, and as soon moved to be moody, and as soon moody to be moved.* |

Romeo and Juliet share a sonnet when they first meet.

GCSE English Literature | Romeo and Juliet

LANGUAGE TECHNIQUES

Shakespeare uses a lot of linguistic and dramatic techniques in *Romeo and Juliet*.

Symbolism

Symbolism is when objects, colours or characters represent concepts. There are plenty of examples of symbolism in *Romeo and Juliet*.

Light

Romeo and Juliet often use light imagery when they describe each other. Romeo comments that Juliet teaches *"the torches to burn bright"* and that she is a *"bright angel"*. This symbolises how their love shines despite the darkness caused by the families' feud.

Night-time

Romeo and Juliet only meet inside or at night: *"Thou know'st the mask of night is on my face"*. This symbolises how their relationship is forbidden and secretive.

Flowers

Shakespeare uses flowers to symbolise both positive and negative concepts within the play.

Flowers can heal with their *"medicine power"*...	but they can also make someone sick: *"Within the infant rind of this small flower / Poison hath residence"*.
Flowers can symbolise shared love: *"This bud of love... / May prove a beauteous flower"*...	but they can also symbolise unrequited love: *"it pricks like thorn"*.
Flowers can symbolise beauty: *"Verona's summer hath not such a flower"*...	but also hide someone's true nature: *"O serpent heart hid with a flowering face!"*

The dual nature of flowers reflects the dual nature of love: love can cause both happiness and sorrow.

Soliloquies

A **soliloquy** is a dramatic technique. It describes a moment in a play where a character speaks their thoughts aloud. Soliloquies are usually directed at the audience, rather than other characters, allowing the audience to understand that character's innermost feelings. For example, Romeo's soliloquy at the start of Act 2, Scene 2 reveals his love for Juliet.

Dramatic irony

Dramatic irony describes when the audience knows more than the characters. For example, the audience know in Act 5, Scene 1 that Juliet has faked her death, but Romeo believes that she really is dead. This increases the tension, as the audience watch Romeo buy a lethal poison because he cannot bear to live without her.

Foreshadowing

Foreshadowing hints at something that will happen later in the play. It can be used to create tension or a sense of unease amongst the audience. For example, Mercutio tells Benvolio that Tybalt is an excellent swordsman. This foreshadows Tybalt stabbing Mercutio in Act 3, Scene 1.

> **Comment:** Foreshadowing is used by Shakespeare to reinforce the idea of fate and destiny. For more on the theme of fate, turn to **page 52**.

Antithesis

Shakespeare frequently uses examples of **antithesis** in *Romeo and Juliet*. This is when two opposing ideas are joined together in a line, for example, *"my only love sprung from my only hate"*. Antithesis can be used to show confusion or conflicted emotions.

> Antithesis and **oxymorons** are similar techniques. Oxymorons are usually just two contrasting words put together, i.e. *"fiend angelical"* whereas antithesis is when contrasting ideas are presented within a longer phrase or sentence.

Imagery

Shakespeare uses **imagery** to convey meaning to the audience in a creative way. Romeo and Juliet's dialogue in Act 2, Scene 2 uses a lot of imagery:

Similes

Juliet says: *"My bounty is as boundless as the sea."* This **simile** expresses how her love for Romeo is as infinite as the ocean.

Metaphors

Romeo says, *"Juliet is the sun"*. He uses this **metaphor** to emphasise how Juliet's beauty lights up the darkness.

Personification

Romeo extends the sun metaphor by using **personification** (when something non-human is given human qualities): *"Arise fair sun, and kill the envious moon"*.

Foil

A **foil** describes a character who is the opposite to another character. Mercutio acts as a foil to Romeo. Where Romeo is romantic and emotional, Mercutio is cynical towards love, and seems only to care about sexual love. See **page 48** for more on attitudes to love.

Puns

Puns are an example of wordplay, and describe a word with a double meaning. Mercutio's dialogue uses a lot of puns, which emphasises his playful and humorous nature. Mercutio even uses puns when he is dying. He tells Romeo, *"Ask for me tomorrow and you shall find me a grave man"*. Mercutio is playing on the word 'grave' which can mean both 'serious' and 'a place where a corpse is buried'.

ACT 1

Act 1 introduces the feud between the Montagues and the Capulets. Romeo and Juliet meet and fall in love.

Act 1, Prologue

The Prologue summarises the whole play in 14 lines. It tells the audience that the play takes place in Verona, and that it centres around two feuding families whose children fall in love.

Comment: The Prologue is written as a **sonnet**. It is recited by the Chorus (a group of actors) and the effect of having multiple voices chanting the Prologue would establish an eerie and unsettling mood at the start of the play.

The Prologue reveals that the lovers will die, but that their deaths help to *"bury their parents' strife"* (end the feud).

Comment: Revealing that Romeo and Juliet die hints that the play is a **tragedy** (see **page 2**). It also introduces the theme of fate (see **page 52**): even though the audience know the two main characters will die, they cannot prevent Romeo and Juliet's deaths.

Act 1, Scene 1

The play begins with two servants from the Capulet family, Sampson and Gregory, discussing their hatred of the Montague family.

Comment: This dialogue reinforces the theme of conflict, and emphasises the families' *"ancient grudge"* from the Prologue. For more on the theme of conflict, turn to **page 54**.

Act 1, Scene 1 establishes the conflict between the two families.

Two servants from the Montague family enter the stage, and draw their swords to fight with Sampson and Gregory.

Comment: This shows just how deep the feud runs: even the servants are prepared to fight, and potentially kill, on behalf of their families. This establishes the hatred that Romeo and Juliet must try to overcome to be together.

Benvolio, a Montague, enters and tries to break up the fight. Tybalt, a Capulet, enters and thinks that Benvolio is involved in the brawl. Benvolio and Tybalt duel.

Comment: Benvolio tries to tell Tybalt that he's not involved in the fight: *"I do but keep the peace"*. Tybalt replies: *"peace? I hate the word, / As I hate hell, all Montagues, and thee"*. Comparing his hatred of Montagues to his hatred of hell emphasises the severity of the feud. For more on the character of Tybalt, turn to **page 44**.

Act 1, Scene 1 continued

Lord and Lady Capulet enter followed by Lord and Lady Montague. Lord Capulet and Lord Montague want to fight each other too. The Prince (the voice of authority in Verona) enters, and demands that everyone put down their weapons.

> **Comment:** The Prince tells the Capulets and the Montagues: *"If ever you disturb our streets again, / Your lives shall pay the forfeit of the peace"* (the Prince threatens to execute anyone caught fighting in the streets). This is an example of **foreshadowing** as the line *"lives shall pay the forfeit of the peace"* hints at the deaths of Mercutio, Tybalt, Paris, Romeo and Juliet.

Everyone except Benvolio and Lord and Lady Montague exit. The Montagues ask Benvolio if they have seen their son, Romeo. They are worried about him, as he has been withdrawn and unhappy recently: *"With tears augmenting the fresh morning's dew"*.

Romeo enters, and the Montagues ask Benvolio to find out why their son is so unhappy.

Romeo tells Benvolio that he is lovesick: he loves a woman who doesn't love him back.

> **Comment:** Romeo uses **oxymorons** such as *"brawling love"*, *"loving hate"* and *"heavy lightness"* to show the confusion he feels at being lovesick. This romantic and emotional dialogue contrasts with the violence and aggression earlier in the scene, and hints that love will also be an important theme. See **page 48** for more.

Act 1, Scene 2

Lord Capulet and Paris enter. Paris, a nobleman, has asked to marry Capulet's daughter, Juliet, even though they have never met. Capulet is hesitant because he thinks his daughter is too young to be married: *"My child is yet a stranger in the world"*. However, he agrees to give his permission, provided his daughter wants to marry Paris.

> **Comment:** Lord Capulet's attitude to his daughter's marriage initially seems quite progressive for the time. He doesn't want her to marry too young, and he wants her to have a choice in who she marries. For more on arranged marriages, turn to **page 3**.

Capulet invites Paris to a masked ball he is hosting that evening.

Capulet gives his servant, Peter, a guest list, and tells him to walk through Verona and invite everyone on the list. Capulet and Paris exit.

Peter admits to the audience that he cannot read. Benvolio and Romeo enter, and Peter asks Romeo to read the guest list for him. Romeo reads the invitation and realises the woman he is in love with, Rosaline, will be at the party.

Benvolio encourages Romeo to go to the party to meet other women to help him get over his unrequited love. Romeo agrees to attend the party.

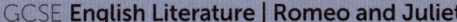

GCSE **English Literature** | Romeo and Juliet

Act 1, Scene 3

Lady Capulet and the Nurse enter, looking for Lady Capulet's daughter, Juliet.

The Nurse, Lady Capulet and Juliet discuss Juliet's possible marriage to Paris.

Comment: The Nurse was Juliet's wet nurse, someone who breastfed another woman's child. Since then, the Nurse has helped raise Juliet and has become a second mother to her.

Juliet enters. The Nurse tells the story of how she stopped breastfeeding Juliet as a baby.

Comment: The Nurse speaks in prose (see **page 9**), which Shakespeare often uses to signal lower-class characters.

The Nurse's story presents her as a comedy character. The story is rambling and funny, with a few rude jokes.

Comment: Shakespeare includes some comical moments early in the play, but there are fewer as the play progresses. Shakespeare didn't want to detract from the tragic ending.

Lady Capulet tells Juliet that Paris wants to marry her, and that he will be at the party that evening.

Comment: Juliet comments that marriage is *"an honour"*. This is an example of a pun, as an 'honour' can mean 'something deserving respect', but it can also mean 'to fulfil an obligation'. Juliet would be expected to honour an arranged marriage to Paris.

Lady Capulet tells Juliet she would *"share all that he doth possess"*, suggesting that the marriage to Paris would financially benefit the Capulet family.

Comment: Lady Capulet tells Juliet how handsome Paris is (*"Verona's summer hath not such a flower"*) but doesn't seem to care whether the couple will be a good match. This suggests that Lady Capulet doesn't prioritise her daughter's happiness.

Juliet agrees to meet Paris, but she is hesitant to make any promises about marrying him.

Act 1, Scene 4

Romeo, Mercutio and Benvolio enter, wearing masks. They are on their way to the Capulets' party. Romeo is still lovesick, commenting: *"I have a soul of lead"*. Mercutio tries to cheer him up, by making rude jokes and encouraging him to find another woman to take his mind off Rosaline.

Comment: This is the audience's first introduction to Mercutio, and he is presented as a fun-loving joker. He's a **foil** to Romeo. For more on the character of Mercutio, turn to **page 42**.

Romeo, Mercutio and Benvolio at the Capulets' masked ball.

Romeo tells Mercutio and Benvolio that he dreamt that the party would result in his *"untimely death"*.

Comment: This is an example of **dramatic irony**, but it also creates suspense. The audience know from the Prologue that Romeo will die, and that his premonition will come true, but they don't know how the party will contribute to his death.

Act 1, Scene 5

Romeo sees Juliet for the first time, and instantly falls in love: *"Did my heart love till now? Forswear it, sight! / For I ne'er saw true beauty till this night"*.

Comment: Despite being infatuated with Rosaline just moments before, Romeo falls in love with Juliet, just by looking at her. This impulsivity is Romeo's **fatal flaw**.

Tybalt recognises Romeo, and is furious that a Montague has gate-crashed the party. Lord Capulet tries to calm Tybalt, and tells him to ignore Romeo. Tybalt insists that the Capulet family is being dishonoured by Romeo's presence, and Lord Capulet tells Tybalt to leave.

Comment: Tybalt later challenges Romeo to a duel as payback for Romeo gate-crashing the Capulets' party. This duel has a devastating impact on Romeo and Juliet's relationship.

Romeo and Juliet meet. They use religious imagery to flirt with each other (*"My lips, two blushing pilgrims, ready stand"*) and they kiss.

Comment: The religious imagery suggests that their attraction is pure and wholesome. Their dialogue also takes the form of a sonnet (see **page 9**), and they complete each other's rhymes. This emphasises their instant connection.

The couple are separated, and they learn each other's identity. They are shocked and upset that they are supposed to be enemies. Juliet says: *"My only love sprung from my only hate!"*

Comment: This scene ends the first act. Revealing that the couple should be enemies creates tension, and the audience wonder if Romeo and Juliet will be able to overcome their families' hatred to be together.

ACT 2

Act 2 establishes Romeo and Juliet's relationship. The audience must be convinced their love is genuine, otherwise the rest of the play isn't believable.

Act 2, Prologue

The Prologue is another sonnet which recaps the most important part of the previous scene: Romeo and Juliet are in love, but their families are enemies, so their relationship faces obstacles.

Comment: The Prologue reiterates this plot point because it's essential to understanding the remainder of the play.

Act 2, Scene 1

Romeo enters, looking for Juliet. He hides when Benvolio and Mercutio enter the stage, looking for him. Mercutio tries to lure Romeo out by talking about Rosaline, but Romeo stays hidden.

Comment: Mercutio jokes about Rosaline's *"quivering thigh"*. His sexual comments contrast with Romeo and Juliet's romantic attitude towards love.

Mercutio and Benvolio give up, and decide to leave the party without Romeo.

Comment: Romeo's decision to stay hidden from his friends suggests he is choosing Juliet over his family. This shows how strongly he feels for her even though they have just met.

Act 2, Scene 2

Romeo sneaks into the Capulets' orchard beneath Juliet's bedroom window. He opens this scene with a **soliloquy**, which allows the audience to hear his true feelings towards Juliet. He uses extended metaphors to compare her to the sun.

Comment: Comparing Juliet to the sun shows her importance to Romeo, as the sun and its light is the source of life.

Juliet speaks a soliloquy that Romeo overhears. She wishes Romeo wasn't a Montague and that she wasn't a Capulet: *"be but sworn my love, / And I'll no longer be a Capulet."*

Comment: The famous line *"Wherefore art thou Romeo?"* doesn't mean "Where are you, Romeo?" it actually means "Why are you Romeo?". Juliet is upset that he is a Montague.

Act 2, Scene 2 continued

Romeo reveals his presence to Juliet. She is concerned what her family will do if they discover him on their property: *"If they do see thee they will murder thee"*.

> **Comment:** Romeo loves Juliet so much he doesn't care that he's putting himself in danger. He tells her: *"And but thou love me, let them find me here. / My life were better ended by their hate."* (If you don't love me, I'd rather they found and killed me.) This introduces their impulsive, intense relationship, and how Romeo would rather die than be without Juliet's love.

Juliet at her balcony.

Juliet asks Romeo if he loves her, and Romeo attempts to *"swear by the sacred moon"* that he does.

> **Comment:** Shakespeare uses dramatic, intense language in this scene to show how deeply Romeo and Juliet have fallen in love. If their love isn't convincing, then the audience won't be invested in the rest of the play.

The Nurse calls for Juliet offstage, and Juliet tries to answer both the Nurse and Romeo. This creates a frenzied atmosphere and heightens the tension: the lovers might be caught at any moment.

> **Comment:** The Nurse's interruption represents how Juliet is torn between her family and her love for Romeo.

Juliet tells Romeo that if he truly loves her, he will arrange for them to be married the next day. Romeo promises to send word about their marriage by nine the next morning and pledges to visit his priest to arrange the ceremony.

Act 2, Scene 3

Friar Lawrence, Romeo's priest, enters. It is dawn, and he is collecting herbs.

In a soliloquy, he remarks how nature can be both good and bad: *"The earth, that's nature's mother, is her tomb. / What is her burying, grave that is her womb."* (Soil can help things grow, but it can also be used to bury things.)

> **Comment:** Friar Lawrence's comments about how things can be both good and bad foreshadows his role within the play: his actions have good intentions, but they end up having terrible consequences. For more on the character of Friar Lawrence, turn to **page 41**.

Friar Lawrence collects herbs.

Act 2, Scene 3 continued

Friar Lawrence comments: *"Within the infant rind of this small flower / Poison hath residence and medicine power"*.

Comment: The Friar's remarks about flowers being able to both kill and heal, foreshadows how Romeo will poison himself at the end of the play, but that his death will help to heal the feud between the two families.

Romeo enters, and tells Friar Lawrence that he has fallen in love with Juliet and that he wants the Friar to marry them today.

The Friar is shocked that Romeo has forgotten Rosaline so quickly: *"here upon thy cheek the stain doth sit / Of an old tear that is not washed off yet."* (There's still a tear stain on your cheek from the tears you cried over Rosaline.) He isn't convinced that Romeo's feelings for Juliet are genuine.

Comment: Romeo confides in the Friar about his forbidden love for Juliet. This suggests that they have a close relationship, and that Romeo trusts the Friar.

Romeo tells Friar Lawrence to stop judging him, and that Juliet, unlike Rosaline, loves him back.

Comment: Romeo's comment highlights his impulsivity. It implies he only wants to marry Juliet because she's the first woman to return his love.

Friar Lawrence agrees to marry the couple because he hopes their union will end the feud between the families, turning their *"rancour to pure love"*, but he warns Romeo about recklessness: *"They stumble that run fast"*.

Comment: Friar Lawrence recognises that Romeo is being impulsive, but he agrees to conduct the wedding ceremony anyway. This suggests that Friar Lawrence has an irresponsible side: he ignores the risks their marriage might create.

Act 2, Scene 4

Mercutio and Benvolio discuss how they haven't seen Romeo since the party the night before. Benvolio tells Mercutio that Tybalt has sent a letter to Romeo, challenging him to a duel for gate-crashing the party.

Romeo enters, and he and Mercutio tease each other with wordplay.

Comment: Mercutio tells Romeo, *"Now art thou sociable. Now art thou Romeo"* implying that this playful, cheerful version of Romeo is the 'real' Romeo. This suggests that being in love with Juliet has made him happy again. However, Romeo doesn't tell his friends the reason for his good mood. He hides his relationship with Juliet, which hints he's drifting apart from his friends.

The Nurse enters, and Mercutio begins to tease her too.

Comment: This scene provides comic relief before tragedy strikes in Act 3.

Act 2, Scene 4 continued

The Nurse pulls Romeo aside, and warns him not to treat Juliet badly or lead her into a *"fool's paradise"*.

> **Comment:** The Nurse cares deeply about Juliet, and doesn't want her to get hurt. Like Friar Lawrence, the Nurse has good intentions, but she is also behaving irresponsibly by encouraging their forbidden and risky relationship.

Romeo assures the Nurse that he has good intentions, and that Juliet should go to confession that afternoon so that Friar Lawrence can marry them.

> **Comment:** As a young, unmarried noblewomen, Juliet couldn't leave the house unaccompanied or without permission. Juliet has to rely on the Nurse to send messages to Romeo on her behalf.

Act 2, Scene 5

Juliet is at home impatiently waiting for the Nurse to bring her news about her wedding to Romeo.

When the Nurse returns, she toys with Juliet, and refuses to tell her about the wedding straightaway.

> **Comment:** The Nurse teases Juliet, which shows their close and playful relationship.

Eventually, the Nurse tells Juliet to go to confession, because *"There stays a husband to make you a wife"*.

The Nurse teases Juliet before telling her the good news.

Act 2, Scene 6

Romeo and Friar Lawrence are waiting for Juliet to arrive. Friar Lawrence is still unsure about the wedding, commenting that, *"violent delights have violent ends"* (intense love can end badly).

> **Comment:** The reference to *"violent ends"* reminds the audience the couple are destined to die.

Juliet enters, and hugs Romeo. The Friar comments that lovers are like *"gossamers"* (spiderwebs).

> **Comment:** The Friar's remark suggests that he's not convinced that their love will stand the test of time, because, like a spiderweb, it seems too fragile.

They leave the stage, so that Friar Lawrence can conduct the ceremony.

> **Comment:** The end of Act 2 ends on a positive note: Romeo and Juliet are in love and head off to be married. This increases the tension because the audience know that something must go wrong for the couple to die by the end of the play.

ACT 3

Act 3 marks a turning point in the play. The positivity at the end of Act 2 is replaced with tragedy when Mercutio and Tybalt are killed, and Romeo is banished.

Act 3, Scene 1

Mercutio, Benvolio and some Montague men enter the stage. Benvolio wants to go home because it's too hot and he's worried they will come across some Capulets.

Comment: Benvolio comments there is *"mad blood stirring"*, which creates a tense atmosphere. He foreshadows the violence and bloodshed that is about to come.

Mercutio and Tybalt fight.

Tybalt and some Capulet men enter. Tybalt is looking for Romeo, but Mercutio provokes him.

Comment: Tybalt and Mercutio's exchange builds the tension. Unlike previous encounters between the Montagues and the Capulets, there is no one to de-escalate the situation.

Romeo enters, and Tybalt insults Romeo, calling him a *"villain"*. Romeo refuses to duel with Tybalt, instead saying *"I have to love thee"*.

Comment: Now that Romeo and Juliet are married, Tybalt is Romeo's cousin by marriage. Romeo doesn't want to fight his own family.

Mercutio decides to fight Tybalt on Romeo's behalf to defend Romeo's honour.

Comment: The sword fights in this scene would be exciting for the audience. They would have been the equivalent of an dramatic action scene in a modern film.

Romeo tries to stop the fight, reminding them that the Prince has forbidden fighting in the streets of Verona, and anyone who disobeys him could be sentenced to death.

Comment: Even the threat of execution doesn't deter Mercutio and Tybalt from fighting. This shows how deep the feud runs.

Tybalt stabs Mercutio, and Tybalt and the other Capulets exit. Mercutio is fatally wounded, and he says, *"ask for me tomorrow, and you will find me a grave man."*

Comment: This is a pun on the word *"grave"* which can mean 'serious' as well as 'a place where a body is buried'.

As Mercutio is dying, he curses the Montagues and the Capulets: *"a plague o' both your houses!"* and exits the stage.

Comment: An innocent man has died. This shows the destructive nature of the feud.

Act 3, Scene 1 continued

Tybalt re-enters, and Romeo is furious that he has killed Mercutio, and he and Tybalt fight.

Comment: Romeo tried to keep the peace, but Mercutio's death has turned him violent. Romeo isn't thinking about the consequences of his actions, he just wants to get revenge. This reinforces Romeo's fatal flaw: his impulsiveness.

Romeo kills Tybalt. Benvolio tells Romeo to flee, because the Prince will have him executed for Tybalt's death.

Comment: Romeo comments: *"I am fortune's fool!"* He believes that fate is tormenting him. This reference to fate reminds the audience of the Act 1 Prologue and the lovers' destiny.

As Romeo exits, the Prince enters with Lord and Lady Capulet and Lord and Lady Montague. Benvolio explains what has happened. Lady Capulet is devastated by Tybalt's death and demands that *"Romeo must not live"*. Lord Montague defends Romeo, saying that Romeo killed Tybalt as an act of revenge for Mercutio's death. The Prince decides to banish Romeo from Verona, and if he comes back *"that hour will be his last"*.

Comment: This creates suspense for the audience. The Capulet family now hate Romeo even more than before, and Romeo's banishment is another obstacle the couple must overcome.

Act 3, Scene 2

Juliet waits impatiently in her room for Romeo to join her so they can consummate their marriage.

Comment: Juliet's excitement may make the audience uneasy: they know that Romeo has just killed Tybalt and has been sentenced to exile, so Juliet's happiness will be short-lived.

The language in Juliet's soliloquy is full of dark imagery: *"Come, civil night, / Thou sober-suited matron, all in black"*.

Comment: Juliet's metaphor describes night as a widow. This foreshadows how Juliet will become a widow herself.

The Nurse enters and tells Juliet, *"He's dead, he's dead, he's dead!"*. Juliet thinks that the Nurse is talking about Romeo.

Comment: This exchange is an example of **dramatic irony**. The audience know that Romeo is alive, but Juliet thinks he's dead.

The Nurse tells Juliet that Tybalt is dead, and Juliet is grief-stricken, thinking both Romeo and Tybalt are dead: *"For who is living if those two are gone?"*

Comment: Juliet's thoughts turn to suicide. This hints how she is prepared to kill herself rather than live without Romeo.

GCSE **English Literature | Romeo and Juliet**

Act 3, Scene 2 continued

The Nurse finally clarifies that Romeo is banished because he killed Tybalt. Juliet then gives a monologue where she uses oxymorons ("*Beautiful tyrant! Fiend angelical!*") to express her confused feelings towards Romeo killing her cousin. But just as suddenly, she is angry at herself for saying negative things about Romeo: *"Oh, what a beast I was to chide him!"*

Comment: Juliet's emotions switch from anger to love showing how conflicted she feels, as she is torn between loyalty to her family and loyalty to Romeo.

Juliet laments that she will not be losing her virginity to Romeo that night and that she will die a virgin: *"death, not Romeo, take my maidenhead"*.

Comment: Juliet is devastated by Romeo's banishment. The audience need to believe that Romeo's banishment is an almost insurmountable obstacle facing the couple.

The Nurse tells Juliet that Friar Lawrence is hiding Romeo, and that she will bring Romeo to her to *"take his last farewell."*

Comment: This is another example of foreshadowing. This will be their *"last farewell"*: it will be the last time the couple will see each other alive.

Act 3, Scene 3

Friar Lawrence is hiding Romeo.

Comment: Friar Lawrence puts himself at risk by hiding Romeo. This shows how devoted he is to Romeo.

Friar Lawrence tells Romeo that he has been banished from Verona. Romeo thinks that banishment is worse than death: *"Ha, banishment! Be merciful, say 'death'"*.

Comment: Romeo is overreacting and behaving irrationally.

The Friar hides Romeo after he is banished.

The Nurse enters, and tells Romeo that Juliet is in her bedroom, crying.

The Friar tries to talk sense into Romeo, reminding him that he and Juliet are still alive, and that he has only been sentenced to exile, not to death. He tells Romeo to visit Juliet, and then flee to Mantua (a town near Verona) until they can announce their marriage and end the feud.

Comment: The Friar takes control of the situation and devises a plan to allow the couple to be together again. He is trying to be sensible and rational.

Romeo agrees to the plan and goes to be with Juliet.

Comment: At the end of this scene, the audience believe that everything could still work out for the couple. This creates a sense of relief and temporarily de-escalates the tension.

Act 3, Scene 4

Lord Capulet, Lady Capulet and Paris enter. The Capulets tell Paris that because of Tybalt's death, they haven't spoken to Juliet about the arranged marriage, but they reassure Paris that they will talk to Juliet tomorrow about an engagement. Lord Capulet believes that Juliet will marry Paris if he tells her to: *"she will be ruled / In all respects by me."*

Comment: This is an example of Elizabethan patriarchal society. Capulet believes he has control over Juliet's actions because he is her father.

Capulet decides, *"O' Thursday, tell her, / She shall be married to this noble earl"*.

Comment: This is another example of **dramatic irony**. The audience knows that Juliet is already married to Romeo, so she cannot marry Paris. This increases the tension for the audience as they wonder how Romeo and Juliet will overcome this new problem.

Act 3, Scene 5

Romeo and Juliet have just spent the night together. Romeo is preparing to leave because he needs to flee before the sun rises. Juliet pleads with him to stay a little longer.

Comment: They talk affectionately, calling each other *"love"*. Their relationship seems genuine and heartfelt.

The Nurse enters and tells Juliet that her mother is on her way to her room.

Comment: This heightens the tension. The audience worry that the couple could be caught.

As Romeo is leaving, Juliet tells him, *"Methinks I see thee now, thou art so low / As one dead in the bottom of a tomb."*

Comment: Juliet has a premonition of looking down on Romeo lying in a tomb. This foreshadows their fate and reminds the audience that their love is doomed.

As Romeo exits, Lady Capulet enters. Juliet pretends that she is mourning Tybalt's death. Lady Capulet is unsympathetic, saying, *"What, wilt thou wash him from his grave with tears? / An if thou couldst, thou couldst not make him live."*

Comment: Lady Capulet thinks that Juliet's sadness is melodramatic. She doesn't try to comfort her daughter, suggesting they do not have a close relationship.

Juliet pretends to be angry towards Romeo to disguise her true feelings for him: *"I never shall be satisfied / With Romeo, till I behold him—dead— / Is my poor heart for a kinsman vexed."*

Comment: Juliet's language is ambiguous. Her mother believes Juliet is saying that she will never be satisfied until Romeo is dead, but the audience can see a different meaning: that Juliet will never be satisfied until she sees Romeo again.

Act 3, Scene 5 continued

Lady Capulet tells Juliet she will marry Paris on Thursday. Juliet is shocked by the news, and says that she doesn't want to marry Paris: *"I swear / It shall be Romeo, whom you know I hate, / Rather than Paris"*.

Comment: The audience recognises the dramatic irony in this statement. Juliet insists she would rather marry Romeo than Paris.

Lord Capulet enters, and he also is unsympathetic to Juliet's sadness over Tybalt's death, calling her a *"conduit"* (fountain). Lady Capulet tells Lord Capulet that Juliet doesn't want to marry Paris.

Comment: Juliet's refusal to obey her parents and marry Paris could be interpreted as sinful. She is breaking one of the Ten Commandments (ten principles that Christians try to live by): honour your father and mother.

Lord Capulet is angry that Juliet has refused, and he threatens to *"drag thee on a hurdle thither"* (drag her to the church on a frame used to drag traitors to execution).

Comment: Capulet's language and punctuation shows his anger. *"How, how, how, how? Chopped logic! What is this?"* The repetition of "how" suggests he's stuttering out of rage, and the exclamation and question marks emphasise his disbelief that Juliet will not marry Paris.

The Nurse and Lady Capulet try to defend Juliet, but Lord Capulet refuses to calm down. Lord Capulet tells Juliet that if she won't marry Paris then he will throw her out of his house and she will *"beg, starve, die in the streets"*.

Comment: As a noblewoman, Juliet would struggle to survive if her family disowned her, as she wouldn't have any way to support herself or make a living.

Lord and Lady Capulet exit, and Juliet asks the Nurse for comfort. The Nurse tells Juliet to marry Paris because *"Romeo is a dishclout to him"* (Romeo is a dishcloth compared to Paris).

Juliet pleads with her father.

Comment: The Nurse is trying to offer practical advice: Paris is wealthy and handsome, whereas Romeo is as good as dead because he is banished. However, the Nurse's practical outlook ignores Juliet's overwhelming love for Romeo.

The Nurse exits, and Juliet admits that she can no longer trust her: *"Go counsellor! / Thou and my bosom henceforth shall be twain."* (Leave then, my confidant. You and my heart are now separated.)

Comment: This is a turning point in the relationship between the Nurse and Juliet. Juliet no longer involves the Nurse in her plan to be with Romeo.

Juliet decides to go Friar Lawrence to ask for his help.

ACT 4

Friar Lawrence devises a plan for Juliet to fake her own death so she doesn't have to marry Paris.

Act 4, Scene 1

Friar Lawrence and Paris discuss the plans for the wedding between Paris and Juliet. Friar Lawrence is openly sceptical about the marriage: *"Uneven is the course. I like it not"*.

Comment: Even though Juliet had refused to marry Paris, her family are proceeding with the wedding. This shows how little respect they have for their daughter's wishes.

Paris claims that the hurried wedding is to distract Juliet from her grief following Tybalt's death: *"her father counts it dangerous / That she do give her sorrow so much sway."*

Comment: It's ironic that Capulet thinks marrying Paris will distract Juliet from her sadness, when, in reality, forcing his daughter to marry Paris is causing her distress.

Juliet enters, and Paris is delighted to see her: *"Happily met, my lady and my wife"*. Paris tries to convince Juliet to say that she loves him: *"I am sure, that you love me"*.

Comment: Paris doesn't seem to notice that Juliet is reluctant to marry him or that she won't make any declaration of love. He's oblivious to how she feels. For more on the character of Paris, see **page 44**.

Juliet takes the poison from Friar Lawrence

Paris exits, and Juliet tells Friar Lawrence that her situation is *"past hope, past cure, past help"* and that she is prepared to kill herself rather than marry Paris.

Comment: Juliet is desperate. Attempting suicide suggests that she is prepared to do anything to prevent the marriage from going ahead.

Friar Lawrence has a plan to help Juliet. He gives her a poison to drink the night before her wedding to Paris. The poison will make her appear to be dead. Her family will lay her body in a crypt, and the Friar will send a message to Romeo who will come to get her, and they will escape to Mantua.

Comment: Friar Lawrence feels obliged to help because of his loyalty to the couple, but he is also partly responsible for their situation because he was the one who married them.

Juliet is delighted with Friar Lawrence's plan and takes the vial of poison.

Act 4, Scene 2

The Capulets are busy preparing for the wedding.

Juliet returns from visiting Friar Lawrence. She pretends that she has changed her mind about the wedding and that she has *"learned me to repent the sin / Of disobedient opposition"*. Capulet is delighted, and decides to bring the wedding forward to Wednesday.

Comment: The Capulets are so eager for the wedding to go ahead, they aren't suspicious about Juliet's sudden change of heart.

Act 4, Scene 3

Juliet and the Nurse are in Juliet's bedroom, picking out her clothes for the wedding the following morning. Juliet asks the Nurse to leave her alone that evening, so that she can pray because her life is *"full of sin"*. Lady Capulet also tries to help Juliet, but she tells them both to leave.

Comment: Juliet doesn't say goodbye to the Nurse or her mother even though it could be the last time she sees them. She feels betrayed by them, and her loyalty lies only with Romeo.

The Nurse exits, and Juliet prepares to drink the poison that Friar Lawrence gave her. Juliet's soliloquy is full of doubt.

Comment: Juliet is 'dead' for the rest of play until she wakes up in Act 5, Scene 3. This soliloquy is Juliet's last significant moment on stage before she dies.

Juliet performs her soliloquy with the bottle of poison.

Juliet is worried that the potion won't work, or that Friar Lawrence has given her a deadly poison. She's also afraid of waking up in the crypt alone where Tybalt *"Lies fest'ring in his shroud"*.

Comment: Juliet is on stage by herself for most of this scene. This represents how she has been deserted by everyone close to her and must face her fears alone.

Eventually, Juliet drinks the potion, saying *"Romeo, Romeo, Romeo! Here's drink. I drink to thee."*

Act 4, Scene 4

It is the morning of the wedding, and the Capulets and the Nurse are busy with the preparations.

Comment: The characters are in a good mood, and there is hustle and bustle. This increases the tension, because the audience wonder when the characters will realise that Juliet is 'dead'.

Capulet tells the Nurse to go to wake Juliet.

Act 4, Scene 5

The Nurse enters and tries to wake Juliet. At first, the Nurse thinks Juliet is asleep, but she soon realises that Juliet is 'dead'.

Capulet, Lady Capulet, Friar Lawrence and Paris enter, and are all told that Juliet is dead. All the characters (except Friar Lawrence), use repetition in their speech. The Nurse says: *"O woe! O woeful, woeful, woeful day!"*

Comment: The characters' grief seems overdramatic and insincere, especially since they didn't seem to care about Juliet when they forced her into marrying Paris.

The Friar tells the other characters to be calm, and scolds them for treating Juliet poorly when she was alive, claiming that, *"'twas your heaven she should be advanced"* (your idea of heaven for her was marrying her off to someone socially superior).

Comment: The Friar accuses the Capulets of using Juliet's marriage to Paris for their own benefit.

Capulet says that all the preparations for the wedding will now be used for Juliet's funeral instead: *"Our bridal flowers serve for a buried corpse"*.

Comment: The flowers that the Capulets bought to celebrate Juliet's wedding will now be used for her funeral. This is another example of how flowers have a dual nature. See **page 10** for more.

A group of musicians (who had expected to play at the wedding) and Peter are the only characters left on stage. The musicians are annoyed that their job playing at the wedding has fallen through. They exchange quips with Peter.

Comment: Shakespeare probably included this humorous moment to give the audience some comic relief ahead of the final act.

GCSE **English Literature** | **Romeo and Juliet**

ACT 5

There are only three scenes in Act 5, and Scene 2 is very short. This increases the pace of the play, and makes it seem as though Romeo and Juliet are hurtling towards their fate.

Act 5, Scene 1

Romeo is in Mantua. In a soliloquy, he claims to have dreamt he was dead, but Juliet brought him back to life with a kiss.

Comment: This foreshadows how Juliet kisses Romeo's corpse in Act 5, Scene 3. It's another example of a premonition of the couple that is associated with death.

Romeo's servant, Balthasar, enters, bringing news from Verona. Balthasar tells Romeo that Juliet is dead: *"Her body sleeps in Capels' monument"*. (Her body lies in the Capulets' crypt.)

Romeo doesn't know about the Friar's plan, so Romeo believes she's actually dead. He reacts by saying, *"Then I defy you, stars!"*

Comment: Romeo believes that fate is conspiring against him. He wants to challenge fate and change the course of his own destiny. Ironically, Romeo's actions result in him fulfilling the predictions of the Prologue.

Romeo asks Balthasar, *"Hast thou no letters to me from the friar?"*. Romeo suspects that Juliet's death could be another of Friar Lawrence's schemes, but Balthasar says, *"No my good lord"*.

Comment: Romeo is so close to recognising that Juliet isn't actually dead, but since he hasn't heard from Friar Lawrence, he assumes her death is real. This instance of dramatic irony increases the tension for the audience.

Romeo decides to go to Verona and kill himself so that he can *"lie with thee tonight"*.

Comment: Romeo loves Juliet so much that he would rather die than live without her.

Romeo buys a vial of poison from the apothecary.

Romeo goes to an apothecary to buy deadly poison. The apothecary is reluctant as selling poison can be punished with the death penalty in Mantua. Romeo mocks the apothecary, telling him *"Art thou so bare and full of wretchedness, / And fear'st to die?"* (How can you be so poor and wretched yet still afraid of death?) Eventually, the apothecary sells the poison to Romeo.

Comment: Romeo bullies the apothecary by calling him worthless and bribes him. This shows how determined Romeo is to buy the poison.

Act 5, Scene 2

Friar Lawrence meets with Friar John, the man who was supposed to deliver a message to Romeo about Juliet's fake death. Friar John tells Friar Lawrence that he didn't deliver the letter.

Friar Lawrence realises that Romeo doesn't know that Juliet's death isn't real, and he decides to go to the Capulets' crypt to be there when Juliet wakes up and bring her back to his cell.

> **Comment:** This scene increases the tension. The audience hope that Friar Lawrence can intercept Romeo and stop him from killing himself, even though they know that Romeo and Juliet are doomed to die.

Act 5, Scene 3

Paris visits Juliet's crypt to lay flowers outside. He hears someone approaching, and hides.

Romeo enters with Balthasar. Romeo intends to open the Capulets' crypt so that he can *"behold my lady's face"*. He tells Balthasar not to interrupt him when he's in the tomb, or else he will *"tear thee joint by joint / And strew this hungry churchyard with thy limbs"*.

> **Comment:** Romeo doesn't want Balthasar to interrupt him taking his own life, but Romeo's grief has turned him irrationally violent.

Romeo begins to force open the crypt, but he is interrupted by Paris. Paris thinks that Romeo means to *"do some villainous shame"* to Tybalt and Juliet's bodies. Paris tries to apprehend Romeo so that he can bring him to the Prince to be executed.

Romeo tells Paris to walk away and *"tempt not a desperate man"* into a fight, but Paris refuses to leave. Romeo kills Paris, and Paris' servant runs away to alert the City Watch.

> **Comment:** Romeo doesn't want to fight Paris, but he won't let anything stand in the way of him dying next to Juliet.

Romeo enters the tomb. He looks at Juliet, and says, *"crimson in thy lips and in thy cheeks, / And death's pale flag is not advanced there."*

> **Comment:** This is an example of dramatic irony. The audience realise the colour is returning to Juliet's complexion because the poison is starting to wear off and she will wake up soon.

Romeo believes that if he kills himself, he will *"shake the yoke of inauspicious stars"* (be free from the cruel hand of fate).

> **Comment:** Romeo thinks he's taking his destiny into his own hands by killing himself. Little does he know that his death is exactly what fate has in store.

GCSE **English Literature** | Romeo and Juliet

Act 5, Scene 3 continued

Romeo drinks the poison and dies next to Juliet. As Romeo dies, Friar Lawrence approaches the crypt, and sees Paris' body.

Juliet wakes up, and asks, *"Where is my Romeo?"*. Friar Lawrence tells her that both Romeo and Paris are dead, and that she should slip away with him before the City Watch arrives. Juliet refuses to leave, and the Friar exits.

> **Comment:** Friar Lawrence abandons Juliet. He's more concerned with protecting himself than helping Juliet.

Juliet notices that Romeo is holding an empty bottle of poison and kisses him to try to take some poison left on his lips.

Juliet hears the City Watch approaching, picks up Romeo's dagger and stabs herself.

> **Comment:** Juliet's death seems rushed: she only speaks two lines before stabbing herself. She wants to end her life before anyone can stop her.

Friar Lawrence tries to persuade Juliet to leave the crypt.

The City Watch arrive with Friar Lawrence (they captured him as he tried to escape). Lord and Lady Capulet, Lord Montague and the Prince arrive.

> **Comment:** As the play draws to a close, most of the surviving characters enter. This allows Shakespeare to tie up all the loose ends all at once. It also shows just how many people have been impacted by the couple's death.

The Friar, along with Balthasar, explain what has happened.

The Prince blames Montague and Capulet for driving their children to kill themselves: *"See what scourge is laid upon your hate, / That heaven finds means to kill your joys with love"*.

Capulet and Montague agree to end the feud. Montague promises to build a *"statue in pure gold"* of Juliet, and Capulet pledges to make a similar statue of Romeo.

> **Comment:** Everything predicted in the Act 1 Prologue has come true, suggesting that a person cannot escape their fate.

Capulet admits that the feud was not worth their children's deaths: *"Poor sacrifices of our enmity"*.

> **Comment:** The end of the play is bittersweet. Although Romeo and Juliet are dead, there is hope that Verona will become a more peaceful place because of their love.

CHARACTERS: ROMEO MONTAGUE

Romeo is a member of the Montague family. He's headstrong, romantic and emotional.

Act 1

Emotional: Romeo's father describes how Romeo adds *"to clouds more clouds with his deep sighs"*. (He sighs so much that his breath creates clouds.)

> **Comment:** This suggests that Romeo feels emotions intensely. This presents him as someone who gets swept away by his feelings, which makes his sudden love for Juliet seem more believable.

Secretive: Romeo's father describes his son as, *"so secret and so close"*.

> **Comment:** Shakespeare establishes Romeo's secretive nature, which helps to explain why he doesn't tell his friends and family about his love for Juliet later in the play.

Romeo falls in love with Juliet instantly.

Eloquent: Romeo uses poetic language to describe his feelings for Rosaline: *"O brawling love, O loving hate, / O anything of nothing first created! O heavy lightness, serious vanity, Misshapen chaos of well-seeming forms!"*

> **Comment:** Romeo uses oxymorons and antithesis to describe his love for Rosaline. The contradictory language shows how confused he is by loving her.

Miserable: Romeo's feelings for Rosaline make him despondent. He compares his unrequited love for her like being *"Shut up in prison, kept without my food"*.

> Rosaline never appears on stage. This makes her seem even more out of reach.

> **Comment:** Romeo uses glum, miserable language when he talks about Rosaline. This contrasts with the bright, positive language he uses to describe Juliet later in the play.

In love: Romeo sees Juliet at the party, and instantly falls in love: *"Did my heart love till now? Forswear it, sight! / For I ne'er saw true beauty till this night."*

> **Comment:** Romeo forgets his feelings towards Rosaline as soon as he sees Juliet. This could be interpreted as Romeo being fickle, suggesting that his love for Rosaline wasn't genuine. However, it could also be interpreted as Romeo's strength of feeling towards Juliet. Romeo was infatuated with Rosaline, so only someone truly special could make him feel this way.

Act 2

Impulsive: Romeo's determined to find Juliet so he sneaks into the Capulets' garden, even though he knows that he could be killed if he's caught.

> **Comment:** Romeo's prepared to put himself in danger to be with Juliet. His impulsive nature makes him behave recklessly. This is Romeo's fatal flaw (see **page 2**).

Lustful: As well as falling in love with Juliet's beauty, he also desires her and wants to have sex with her. He wants her to *"Cast... off!"* her virginity.

> **Comment:** As well as being a romantic, emotional character, Romeo also has sexual desires. This presents his love for Juliet as something genuine and tangible, rather than just idealised.

Witty: In Act 2, Scene 4, Romeo exchanges witty banter with Mercutio. Their jokes show the audience Romeo's fun-loving, humorous side.

> **Comment:** After they exchange jokes, Mercutio says, *"Now thou art Romeo"*. This hints that Romeo's playful side is the real Romeo, rather than the moping, lovesick Romeo at the start of Act 1. This suggests that being in love with Juliet brings out his true nature.

Act 3

Passive: When Tybalt tries to start a fight with him in Act 3, Scene 1, Romeo refuses to fight back. He tries to prevent Tybalt and Mercutio from fighting: *"Tybalt, Mercutio! The Prince expressly hath / Forbidden bandying in Verona streets"*.

> **Comment:** Romeo refuses to fight because Tybalt is now his cousin by marriage. Romeo acknowledges that Juliet has *"softened valour's steel"* (made him more peaceful).

Vengeful: After Tybalt kills Mercutio, Romeo is full of rage: *"fire-eyed fury be my conduct now"*.

> **Comment:** Romeo kills Tybalt to avenge Mercutio's death. This shows Romeo's loyalty to Mercutio, as well as how the feud can turn even peaceful characters violent.

The feud causes Romeo to kill Tybalt.

Melodramatic: When Friar Lawrence tells Romeo that the Prince has banished him from Verona, Romeo says: *"Ha, banishment! Be merciful, say 'death'"*. Romeo thinks that being banished is a more severe punishment than death.

> **Comment:** Romeo is so upset about being banished because he will be separated from Juliet.

Romeo doesn't appear in Act 4.

Act 5

Devastated: When Romeo believes that Juliet is dead, he decides to kill himself rather than live without her.

Comment: Romeo doesn't debate whether suicide is the right course of action. He instantly decides that he will buy poison and die next to Juliet's body. Previously, when Romeo needed help, he turned to Friar Lawrence. However, now he is alone he has no one to calm him down and offer rational advice.

Wild: When Romeo goes to see Juliet in the Capulets' crypt, he won't let anything stand in his way. He threatens to tear Balthasar apart *"joint by joint"* if Balthasar tries to stop him, and he kills Paris when Paris tries to apprehend him.

Romeo holds Juliet in the crypt.

Comment: Romeo's grief has made him *"savage, wild"*. Nothing else matters in the world except killing himself next to Juliet. Romeo's language also changes. He describes the door to Juliet's tomb as a *"detestable maw"* and *"rotten jaw"*. This contrasts with the beautiful, romantic imagery he uses elsewhere in the play, and emphasises Romeo's morbid state of mind.

Defiant: Romeo believes that killing himself will *"shake the yoke of inauspicious stars"* and set himself free from fate.

Comment: Romeo implies fate is to blame for Juliet's death. He doesn't acknowledge any responsibility for his part in the couple's downfall.

Read the following extract from Act 1, Scene 1. At this point in the play, Romeo confesses to Benvolio that he is lovesick.

BENVOLIO
    What sadness lengthens Romeo's hours?

ROMEO
    Not having that, which, having, makes them short.

BENVOLIO
    In love?

ROMEO
    Out--

BENVOLIO
    Of love?

ROMEO
    Out of her favour, where I am in love.

BENVOLIO
    Alas, that love, so gentle in his view,
    Should be so tyrannous and rough in proof!

ROMEO
    Alas, that love, whose view is muffled still,
    Should, without eyes, see pathways to his will!
    Where shall we dine? O me! What fray was here?
    Yet tell me not, for I have heard it all.
    Here's much to do with hate, but more with love.
    Why, then, O brawling love! O loving hate!
    O any thing, of nothing first create!
    O heavy lightness! Serious vanity!
    Mis-shapen chaos of well-seeming forms!
    Feather of lead, bright smoke, cold fire, sick health!
    Still-waking sleep, that is not what it is!
    This love feel I, that feel no love in this.
    Dost thou not laugh?

Starting with this dialogue, explore how far Shakespeare presents Romeo as a male character with strong emotions.

Write about:
- how Shakespeare presents Romeo in this extract
- how far Shakespeare presents Romeo as a male character with strong emotions in the play as a whole. [30 + 4 marks]

Your answer may include:

AO1 — show understanding of the text
- In this extract, Romeo is lovesick. His unrequited love for Rosaline has made him miserable.
- Romeo thinks that Benvolio finds his love for Rosaline funny: "Dost thou not laugh?". This suggests that Benvolio doesn't empathise with Romeo's strong feelings.
- Later in Act 1, Romeo instantly falls in love with Juliet, suggesting that he is impulsive, and falls in love quickly.
- Romeo is also presented as a character who can be quick to anger. When Tybalt stabs Mercutio, Romeo kills Tybalt in revenge without thinking about the consequences.
- When Romeo believes Juliet is dead, he behaves impulsively, deciding to kill himself rather than live without her.

AO2 — show understanding of the writer's language choices
- The monologue in the extract helps to convey Romeo's emotions to the audience. He talks at length about his feelings.
- Some of Romeo's lines in the extract are rhyming couplets, but others do not rhyme. This suggests that Romeo's feelings towards Rosaline, just like the rhyme scheme, are incomplete.
- Shakespeare uses exclamation marks to suggest that the actor playing Romeo should deliver these lines with strong emotion.
- Shakespeare uses oxymorons ("heavy lightness! Serious vanity") to show Romeo's confusion at being lovesick. This contrasts with Romeo's language later in the play when he is in love with Juliet. His dialogue becomes more positive, using symbolism of light to describe Juliet.

AO3 — relate the play to the context
- The play is a tragedy, and Romeo's impulsivity is his fatal flaw which leads to his death.
- Romeo's overly romantic nature would have been unusual for men at this time. Shakespeare subverts stereotypical male traits to present him as a romantic and emotional character.
- The play is set in Italy, so audiences would have expected the protagonist to behave intensely because Italy's hot weather was associated with passion.
- The oxymorons "brawling love" and "loving hate" represent the dual theme of love and conflict that run through the play.

This answer should be marked in accordance with the levels-based mark scheme on page 61.

Make sure your answer to this question is in paragraphs and full sentences. Bullet points have been used in this example answer to suggest some information you could include, but these suggestions are not exhaustive. There are four marks available for spelling, punctuation and grammar, so make sure you read through your answer carefully, correcting any mistakes.

CHARACTERS: JULIET CAPULET

Juliet is the only daughter of the Capulets. She's just 13 when she meets Romeo and falls in love.

Act 1

Comment: At the start of Act 1, Juliet conforms to stereotypical 16th-century female behaviour. She seems to be submissive, obedient and modest. When she meets Romeo, Juliet rebels against these stereotypes, and becomes more assertive, disobedient and sexual. For more on gender roles, turn to **page 58**.

Juliet's parents expect her to be a wife and mother.

Young: Juliet is a few weeks away from her 14th birthday. Despite this, Juliet's mother encourages her to marry and have children: *"Younger than you / Here in Verona, ladies of esteem / Are already mothers"*.

Comment: Today, expecting a girl to be married with children by 13 seems unreasonable, but in the 14th century (when the play is set) it would have been fairly common. Lady Capulet believes that it is Juliet's duty to be a wife and mother.

Reluctant: When Lady Capulet tells her about Paris' marriage proposal, Juliet seems reluctant. She's willing to meet Paris, but she doesn't seem excited by the prospect of getting married.

Comment: Juliet is prepared to obey her parents initially. She knows that she is expected to have an arranged marriage, and as the only child of the Capulets, there would have been a lot of pressure on her to marry a man who would benefit the Capulet family.

Witty: She flirts with Romeo at the party, and matches his wordplay, showing her intelligence.

Comment: Juliet isn't intimidated by Romeo, and quickly establishes herself as his equal.

Impulsive: Juliet kisses Romeo and falls in love with him just as quickly as he falls in love with her.

Comment: Juliet's willingness to kiss Romeo would have been quite scandalous to Shakespearian audiences. Women, especially young nobles, would have been expected to be chaste (not showing any sexual desire) and innocent.

Act 2

In love: Juliet confesses her love for Romeo: *"So Romeo would, were he not Romeo called, / Retain that dear perfection which he owes / Without that title."*

> **Comment:** Juliet admits she loves Romeo in a soliloquy. This makes her feelings seem more genuine because she thinks that no one can hear her.

Self-aware: Juliet acknowledges that Romeo might think her *"too quickly won"* (she's fallen in love too quickly).

> **Comment:** In Shakespearian times, noblemen usually attempted to 'woo' women. At first, the woman might act disinterested and cold, so that the man has to work harder to win her over.

Juliet recognises that Romeo might think she's being too eager. However, this makes their love seem more genuine. Juliet doesn't want to pretend or play games: she wants Romeo to know her true feelings.

Assertive: Juliet is the first to suggest marriage: *"If thy bent of love be honourable. / Thy purpose marriage, send me word tomorrow."* (If you truly love me, you will marry me and let me know when tomorrow.)

> **Comment:** When Lady Capulet asks Juliet about marriage in Act 1, Scene 3, Juliet says marriage is *"an honour that I dream not of"* (an honour I haven't given much thought to). After she meets Romeo, she changes her mind and is prepared to marry him the next day.

Intense: Juliet tells Romeo if he were her pet bird, *"I should kill thee with much cherishing"*.

> **Comment:** Romeo and Juliet's language often references death. This foreshadows the play's unhappy ending, and reminds the audience that their love is doomed.

Juliet falls in love with Romeo very quickly.

Act 3

Passionate: Juliet is eager for Romeo to *"Leap to these arms"* so they can have sex.

> **Comment:** Juliet's sexual desire would have been quite shocking to Shakespearian audiences, but her eagerness for physical intimacy shows how their love is real and tangible, not just formal and distant.

Emotional: When Juliet finds out that Romeo killed Tybalt she's conflicted: *"Beautiful tyrant! Fiend angelical! / Dove-feathered raven, wolvish ravening lamb!"*

> **Comment:** Juliet's use of oxymorons shows her confused feelings towards Romeo: she loves him, but she's upset that he's killed her cousin. These oxymorons also mimic those used by Romeo in Act 1, Scene 1. This similarity in their speech connects their characters further.

Act 3 continued

Melodramatic: Like Romeo, Juliet is devastated that Romeo has been banished: *"that one word 'banishèd' / Hath slain ten thousand Tybalts."*

Comment: Both Juliet and Romeo overreact to his banishment, showing how desperate they are to be together. Shakespeare also uses Romeo's banishment to create tension: it's an obstacle that the lovers must overcome to be together.

Lady Capulet turns on Juliet when she refuses to marry Paris.

Deceptive: Juliet pretends her sadness about Romeo's banishment is sadness over Tybalt's death. She tells her mother, *"let me weep for such a feeling loss"*.

Comment: Juliet tells her mother that Romeo *"doth grieve my heart"*. This is an example of dramatic irony: Lady Capulet thinks that Romeo makes Juliet sad because he killed Tybalt, but Juliet actually means that Romeo makes her sad because he's been banished.

Rebellious: Juliet refuses to marry Paris, telling Lord Capulet: *"He shall not make me a joyful bride"*.

Comment: Capulet is furious at Juliet's disobedience, but even when her father verbally abuses her (calling her a *"wretched puling fool"*) Juliet refuses to back down.

Desperate: Juliet would rather die than marry Paris: *"If all else fail, myself have power to die"*.

Comment: Juliet would rather die than betray Romeo by marrying another man. Juliet is loyal to Romeo, even though it makes her life much more difficult.

Uncertain: Before Juliet drinks the Friar's poison, she admits how scared she is. She's afraid the poison won't work, as well as being scared that the poison will kill her. She fears waking up in the crypt with the *"bones / Of all my buried ancestors"*.

Comment: Juliet's soliloquy shows that she is prepared to face her deepest fears for love.

Act 5

Brave: Juliet wakes up in the tomb, and Friar Lawrence tells her that Romeo is dead. The Friar urges her to leave with him, but she refuses, choosing to kill herself rather than live without Romeo.

Comment: During her soliloquy in Act 4, Scene 3, Juliet comments that she is afraid of being in the crypt by herself with Tybalt's *"fest'ring"* corpse and her ancestors' bones. Even though her worst fear has come true, she refuses to leave Romeo. This shows her devotion.

Read the following extract from Act 3, Scene 2. At this point in the play, Juliet is waiting for Romeo to come to her on their wedding night.

JULIET

    Gallop apace, you fiery-footed steeds,
    Towards Phoebus' lodging: such a wagoner
    As Phaethon would whip you to the west,
    And bring in cloudy night immediately.
    Spread thy close curtain, love-performing night,
    That runaway's eyes may wink and Romeo
    Leap to these arms, untalk'd of and unseen.
    Lovers can see to do their amorous rites
    By their own beauties; or, if love be blind,
    It best agrees with night. Come, civil night,
    Thou sober-suited matron, all in black,
    And learn me how to lose a winning match,
    Play'd for a pair of stainless maidenhoods:
    Hood my unmann'd blood, bating in my cheeks,
    With thy black mantle; till strange love, grown bold,
    Think true love acted simple modesty.
    Come, night; come, Romeo; come, thou day in night;
    For thou wilt lie upon the wings of night
    Whiter than new snow on a raven's back.
    Come, gentle night, come, loving, black-brow'd night,
    Give me my Romeo; and, when he shall die,
    Take him and cut him out in little stars,
    And he will make the face of heaven so fine
    That all the world will be in love with night
    And pay no worship to the garish sun.

Starting with this moment in the play, explore how Shakespeare presents the relationship between Romeo and Juliet.

Write about:
- how Shakespeare presents their relationship in this extract
- how Shakespeare presents their relationship in the play as a whole. [30 + 4 marks]

Your answer may include:

AO1 — show understanding of the text
- *In this extract, Juliet is waiting impatiently for Romeo so that they can consummate their marriage. This shows how physical love is just as important to Juliet as romantic love.*
- *Throughout the play, Shakespeare presents their love as passionate and impulsive. They fall in love instantly, and are married within hours of meeting each other.*
- *They are prepared to take enormous risks to be together. In the extract, unbeknownst to Juliet, Romeo has been banished, and he risks death by staying in Verona to be with her.*
- *Ultimately, they fulfil their destiny of "star-crossed" lovers, and they would rather die than be without each other.*

AO2 — show understanding of the writer's language choices
- *Shakespeare uses this soliloquy to reveal Juliet's innermost thoughts to the audience, showing how she genuinely feels about Romeo.*
- *Juliet wants night to fall: "Come, civil night". Romeo and Juliet's meetings often take place at night. This symbolises the secretive and forbidden nature of their love.*
- *Shakespeare's language foreshadows the couple's eventual demise. Juliet describes night as a widow ("a sober-suited matron") which hints at Juliet briefly becoming a widow in Act 5.*
- *Juliet's line: "when he shall die, / Take him and cut him out in little stars" reminds the audience that Romeo will die, and the reference to "stars" hints at the theme of fate.*

AO3 — relate the play to the context
- *Juliet's sexual desires would have been quite shocking to the audience, as women were expected to be chaste. Her desires make their love seem more tangible and real. Their love isn't just romantic and idealised.*
- *Their relationship is intertwined with the theme of fate. The audience know from the Prologue that they are doomed to die.*
- *The theme of conflict and the backdrop of the families' feud makes their love seem stronger and more romantic because there are obstacles that they must overcome.*

This answer should be marked in accordance with the levels-based mark scheme on page 61.

Make sure your answer to this question is in paragraphs and full sentences. Bullet points have been used in this example answer to suggest some information you could include, but these suggestions are not exhaustive. There are four marks available for spelling, punctuation and grammar, so make sure you read through your answer carefully, correcting any mistakes.

CHARACTERS: FRIAR LAWRENCE

Friar Lawrence is a father figure to Romeo. Although he tries to help the couple, his actions lead to tragedy.

Comment: The Friar is a man of God who offers spiritual and religious guidance to the people of Verona, so the other characters trust and respect his wisdom.

Act 2

Trusted: Romeo tells the Friar about his forbidden love for Juliet.

Comment: Romeo confides in the Friar, suggesting they are close. The Friar also calls Romeo *"pupil mine"* and *"good son"*, which shows they have a caring relationship.

Willing: Friar Lawrence recognises that Romeo and Juliet's marriage could end the feud between the two families, so he's prepared to marry them to *"turn your households' rancour to pure love"*.

Comment: The Friar wants to exploit Romeo and Juliet's union for the benefit of Verona. Although his intentions are good, he's not thinking about what's best for Romeo and Juliet.

Friar Lawrence has good intentions, but his actions end in disaster.

Wary: The Friar urges Romeo to be careful: *"Wisely and slow; they stumble that run fast"*.

Comment: The Friar often advises other characters to be cautious, but he doesn't seem to follow his own advice; his plans are often risky and irresponsible.

Act 3

Loyal: Friar Lawrence hides Romeo after he has been banished from Verona.

Comment: The Friar puts himself at risk by harbouring a criminal.

Act 4

Irresponsible: The Friar gives Juliet the poison which mimics death.

Comment: The Friar's plan is risky and dangerous. The poison he gives Juliet escalates the situation, and ultimately ends with the couple's double suicide.

Act 5

Cowardly: When he realises that the City Watch are approaching, Friar Lawrence tries to run away (*"I dare no longer stay"*) and he abandons Juliet in the tomb.

Comment: The Friar tries to run away from the City Watch to avoid getting himself into trouble. He chooses to protect his reputation rather than try to help Juliet.

CHARACTERS: MERCUTIO

Mercutio is a nobleman of Verona. He is always looking out for his friend, Romeo, but he hides his protective nature behind jokes and insults.

Act 1

Crude: Mercutio's dialogue is full of rude jokes: *"Prick love for pricking"* (*"Prick"* is another word for 'penis'.)

Comment: Mercutio's humour often uses puns, words which have a double (often sexual) meaning. Mercutio's sexual view of love contrasts with Romeo's romantic outlook.

Outgoing: He's talkative and wants to have a good time. He tells Romeo, *"we must have you dance"*.

Comment: Mercutio attempts to distract Romeo from his lovesick feelings towards Rosaline with jokes, and he encourages Romeo to enjoy himself and flirt with other women at the party.

Mercutio is a joker who provides much of the play's comic relief.

Act 2

Mocking: After the Capulets' party, Mercutio tries to find Romeo by calling out insults, and making fun of Romeo's romantic nature: *"Pronounce but 'love' and 'dove'"*.

Comment: Mercutio teasing Romeo suggests that they have a close, playful relationship.

Act 3

Aggressive: Mercutio deliberately tries to antagonise Tybalt in Act 3, Scene 1, calling him a *"ratcatcher"* (Tibalt was the name of a cat in a popular story).

Despite being close, Romeo doesn't tell Mercutio about Juliet. This could be because Romeo doesn't trust Mercutio, or because Mercutio wouldn't understand their love.

Comment: Aggression was seen as a 'typical' male characteristic. When Romeo refuses to fight Tybalt, Mercutio accuses Romeo of being *"dishonourable"*. For more on gender stereotypes, turn to **page 58**.

Unforgiving: As Mercutio lays dying, he curses both the Montagues and the Capulets: *"A plague o' both your houses!"*

Comment: Shakespeare presents Mercutio as a funny, likeable character. This makes his unnecessary death seem even more tragic to the audience.

CHARACTERS: THE NURSE

The Nurse helped to raise Juliet, so they have a very close relationship.

Act 1

Talkative: In Act 1, Scene 3, the Nurse has a monologue recalling how she stopped breastfeeding Juliet.

Comment: The Nurse's chatty, rambling monologue is in prose (see **page 9**). Most of the play's comical or light-hearted moments are written in prose.

Crude: The Nurse often makes sexual jokes. She remembers how Juliet hit her head when she was a baby and had a bump the size of a *"cockerel's stone"* (rooster's testicle).

Comment: The Nurse is a humorous character who brings comic relief to her scenes. Her silly nature also hints that she might not be a very responsible or sensible influence on Juliet.

The Nurse is warm and loving.

Loving: The Nurse cares deeply about Juliet. Her *"wish"* is to see Juliet married, and she uses affectionate pet names for Juliet such as *"lamb"* and *"ladybird"*.

Comment: The Nurse seems to be more of a mother figure to Juliet than Lady Capulet. For more on Juliet's relationship with her mother, turn to **page 46**.

Act 2

Trustworthy: Juliet trusts the Nurse to send messages to Romeo about their wedding.

Comment: Juliet confides in the Nurse suggesting they have a close relationship. The Nurse also puts herself at risk for Juliet by going behind Lord and Lady Capulet's backs.

Act 3

Fickle: After Romeo is banished, the Nurse encourages Juliet to marry Paris instead. The Nurse believes that Paris *"excels"* Romeo, and that Romeo is as good as dead.

Comment: Although the Nurse is only looking out for Juliet, Juliet feels betrayed by the Nurse, calling her a *"wicked fiend"*.

Act 4

Devastated: The nurse is devastated when Juliet is 'dead': *"Never was seen so black a day as this"*.

Comment: The Nurse also uses repetition in her dialogue: *"O woe! O woeful, woeful, woeful day!"*. She's so distraught she can't communicate her feelings properly.

CHARACTERS: TYBALT AND PARIS

Tybalt is a Capulet and Juliet's cousin. He's aggressive and quick to anger. Paris is a handsome, wealthy nobleman who gets engaged to Juliet.

Tybalt

Act 1

Aggressive: When Benvolio tries to break up the street brawl, Tybalt wants to fight: *"Turn thee, Benvolio. Look upon thy death"*.

> **Comment:** From the opening scene, Shakespeare presents Tybalt as a violent character who provokes the feud.

Quick to anger: Tybalt is furious when he discovers Romeo at the Capulets' party, and is prepared to fight him, even though Romeo isn't causing any trouble.

> **Comment:** Lord Capulet convinces Tybalt not to start a fight. This suggests that Tybalt is more concerned with the feud than his uncle.

Tybalt kills Mercutio.

Act 3

Deceitful: Tybalt stabs Mercutio under Romeo's arm. He doesn't fight fair.

> **Comment:** Tybalt didn't want to beat Mercutio in a duel: he wanted to kill him.

Paris

Act 1

Respectful: Unlike Romeo, Paris asks Juliet's father for her hand in marriage. It's important to Paris that Juliet's family approve of the match.

> **Comment:** Asking a father for permission to marry his daughter was expected. It was seen a mark of respect since daughters were considered their father's property.

Act 2

A catch: Paris is polite, handsome, wealthy and seems genuinely happy to marry Juliet.

> **Comment:** Even though Paris is a catch and her parents approve of him, Juliet still chooses to be with Romeo. This shows how strong Juliet's feelings are towards Romeo.

Act 5

Devoted: Paris dies trying to protect Juliet's body from Romeo. Paris' dying wish is for his body to be laid next to Juliet's.

> **Comment:** Paris loves Juliet so much he's willing to die for her, even when Romeo gives him an opportunity to run away. His death is unnecessary: another life claimed by the feud.

CHARACTERS: BENVOLIO AND THE PRINCE

Benvolio is Romeo's cousin and friend. He tries to keep the peace. The Prince is the voice of authority in Verona. He's related to both Mercutio and Paris.

Benvolio

Act 1

Peaceful: Benvolio tries to break up the fight in Act 1, Scene 1: *"Part fools! / Put up your swords. You know not what you do"*.

Comment: Although he's a Montague (and therefore involved in the families' feud), Benvolio tries to avoid conflict.

Sympathetic: He listens to Romeo when he's in love with Rosaline and he tries to cheer him up by encouraging him to *"Examine other beauties"*.

Comment: Although he's a good friend to Romeo, Romeo never confides in Benvolio about Juliet.

Benvolio tries to stop Romeo from fighting Tybalt.

Act 3

Loyal: After Romeo kills Tybalt, Benvolio stays behind to tell the Prince that Romeo tried to stop the fighting with *"calm look, knees humbly bowed"*.

Comment: Benvolio defends Romeo's actions to the Prince to convince him to show mercy.

The Prince

Act 1

Outraged: The Prince is angry that the feud causes so much violence in Verona. He threatens to execute anyone who disturbs the peace.

Comment: Even though the Prince is the most powerful man in Verona, even he cannot end the feud. This shows how uncontrollable the conflict has become.

Act 5

Regretful: The Prince acknowledges that the feud led to the deaths of his *"kinsmen"*. (The Prince was related to both Mercutio and Paris.)

Comment: Even people who weren't related to the Capulets or the Montagues became victims. This shows how brutal the feud was.

CHARACTERS: THE CAPULETS

Lord Capulet is a changeable man. He can be reasonable and peaceful, but he has a short fuse. Lady Capulet is a cold-hearted, distant mother.

Lord Capulet

Act 1

Reasonable: In Act 1, Capulet seems protective of Juliet. He's happy for Paris to try to *"woo"* Juliet, but he warns Paris that Juliet has a *"choice"*, and she may turn him down.

Comment: Capulet's attitude towards his daughter's betrothal to Paris changes dramatically throughout the play.

Act 3

Controlling: When Juliet refuses to marry Paris, her father is furious. He verbally abuses Juliet, and threatens to disown her.

Comment: Capulet's reaction demonstrates the patriarchal nature of Elizabethan society. Capulet expects complete obedience from Juliet, especially since he views her as his property.

Lord Capulet is devastated when Juliet 'dies'.

Lady Capulet

Act 1

Cold: Lady Capulet doesn't have a very close relationship with her daughter. Juliet calls her mother *"Madam"*, and Juliet doesn't confide in her about her relationship with Romeo.

Comment: Juliet's formal and distant relationship with her mother contrasts with her loving and trusting relationship with the Nurse.

Shallow: Lady Capulet thinks Paris is a good match because he's wealthy and handsome. She doesn't care if they'll be happy together, she just wants the marriage to benefit the family.

Comment: Marrying for status was very common in the 16th century, so Lady Capulet's attitude wouldn't have been unusual to Elizabethan audiences.

Act 3

Unsympathetic: Lady Capulet thinks Juliet is overreacting about Tybalt's death: *"much of grief shows still some want of wit"*. (Too much grief makes you look silly.)

Comment: Her comments maker her seem cold and heartless.

Vengeful: Lady Capulet wants to avenge Tybalt's death by poisoning Romeo.

Comment: Lady Capulet is unforgiving and prepared to intensify the feud by having Romeo killed.

CHARACTERS: THE MONTAGUES

The Montagues are Romeo's mother and father. Just like the Capulets, they don't know about Romeo and Juliet's relationship until it's too late.

Lord Montague

Act 1

Violent: Lord Montague tries to fight Capulet in Act 1, Scene 1, but his wife holds him back.

Comment: Shakespeare establishes the violence of the families' feud from the very first scene to show why Romeo and Juliet must keep their relationship a secret.

Concerned: Lord Montague knows that something's not right with Romeo in Act 1, Scene 1, and he asks Benvolio to find out what is troubling his son.

Comment: Romeo doesn't confide in his parents, suggesting their relationship isn't close.

Act 5

Peaceful: After he discovers that Romeo and Juliet are dead, Lord Montague promises to build a *"statue in pure gold"* of Juliet.

Comment: The reconciliation between Montague and Capulet gives the audience hope that the feud has finally ended.

Lady Montague

Act 1

Peaceful: Lady Montague holds her husband back when he tries to join the fight in Act 1, Scene 1. She warns him: *"Thou shalt not stir one foot to seek a foe."*

She's also pleased that Romeo wasn't involved in the fight: *"Right glad I am he was not at this fray."*

Comment: The safety of her husband and son are more important to her than the feud.

Lady Montague and Benvolio.

Act 5

Heart-broken: When Romeo is banished from Verona, Lady Montague dies from grief: *"Grief of my son's exile hath stopped her breath"*.

Comment: Lady Montague is another victim of the feud.

THEMES: LOVE

Shakespeare presents different types of love in the play: unrequited love, romantic love, sexual love and formal love.

Rosaline

Before Romeo and Juliet meet, Romeo is infatuated with Rosaline. Romeo's love for Rosaline is unrequited (i.e. Rosaline doesn't love Romeo back).

Comment: In medieval times, men and women who were interested in each other were expected to behave in a certain way. The man would try to woo the woman, but she would act distant at first to make the man work harder for her affection. It's not clear whether Rosaline isn't interested in Romeo at all, or whether she's playing hard to get. This reluctance contrasts with Juliet's eagerness, as Juliet admits she is *"too quickly won"*.

Romeo's love for Rosaline has several purposes:

- It introduces Romeo as a romantic character who wants to be loved. This makes it more believable when he falls in love with Juliet so quickly.
- Rosaline never appears on stage, which makes Romeo's love for her seem idealised and distant. However, the audience see how Romeo and Juliet behave when they are together which makes their love seems passionate and realistic.
- Romeo's infatuation with Rosaline makes him miserable, whereas his love for Juliet makes him happy. This suggests that Juliet's love has a positive influence on Romeo.

Comment: It could also be argued that Romeo switching his affection from Rosaline to Juliet makes him seem insincere and that Romeo just falls for anyone who loves him back.

Romeo and Juliet

Romeo and Juliet's love is powerful and intense. They make each other happy, but their love makes them behave irrationally.

- They get married within hours of meeting each other, even though their families are enemies.
- They put themselves, and others, at risk. Romeo sneaks into the Capulets' gardens to find Juliet, even though he might be killed if he's caught.
- They would rather die than spend their lives apart.

Comment: It's not clear whether Romeo and Juliet act this way because their love is so intense, or whether it's their impulsive natures which drive them to behave recklessly. Romeo and Juliet are also very young, so their intense love could just be interpreted as immaturity.

Romeo and Juliet's love is passionate but destructive.

Romeo and Juliet continued

Romantic love

When Romeo and Juliet first meet, their lines form a **sonnet** (see **page 9**) a type of love poetry, and they finish each other's rhymes. This emphasises their romantic love and reinforces the idea that they have a deep connection and are meant to be together.

Doomed love

Shakespeare often uses dark imagery when talking about Romeo and Juliet's love. For example, Friar Lawrence says: *"These violent delights have violent ends"*. This emphasises their intense feelings for one another, but also reminds the audience that their love is doomed.

Sexual love

As well as their deep, emotional connection, Romeo and Juliet also express their sexual love for each other. For example, before they sleep together, Juliet says she has been *"sold"* (married) but *"Not yet enjoyed"*.

This makes their love seem more passionate: it's not just an idealised, distant relationship, there's also sexual desire.

The Nurse

The Nurse uses sexual imagery in her dialogue, reminding the audience that it's not just men who experience sexual desire. The Nurse believes Juliet should *"seek happy nights to happy days"*. The Nurse wants Juliet to be sexually satisfied as well as emotionally satisfied.

Paris

Paris pursues Juliet in a conventional, formal way.

- Paris asks Juliet's father for his permission to woo Juliet. This would have been expected at the time, as daughters were seen as their fathers' property.
- Paris hasn't met Juliet before he proposes marriage. This suggests that their match is practical, rather than emotional. Paris is a wealthy nobleman who is related to the Prince, so their marriage would offer the Capulets money and power.
- When Juliet and Paris finally meet in Act 4, Scene 1, Paris tries to flatter Juliet, but she is reserved. This contrasts with Romeo and Juliet's first meeting, where they are swept up in their feelings for each other.

Mercutio

Mercutio is cynical towards romantic love, and instead focuses on sexual love:

- Mercutio thinks that Romeo should sleep with other women to help him forget Rosaline.
- Mercutio often makes sexual references. He jokes that Romeo bows *"in the hams"* (thrusts his upper legs, i.e. has sex).

Comment: Mercutio's focus on sex makes Romeo and Juliet's relationship seem purer and more genuine because they have an emotional connection, not just a physical connection.

GCSE **English Literature** | Romeo and Juliet

Read the following extract from Act 1, Scene 5. At this point in the play, Romeo and Juliet have just met for the first time.

ROMEO

[To JULIET]
If I profane with my unworthiest hand
This holy shrine, the gentle fine is this:
My lips, two blushing pilgrims, ready stand
To smooth that rough touch with a tender kiss.

JULIET

Good pilgrim, you do wrong your hand too much,
Which mannerly devotion shows in this;
For saints have hands that pilgrims' hands do touch,
And palm to palm is holy palmers' kiss.

ROMEO

Have not saints lips, and holy palmers too?

JULIET

Ay, pilgrim, lips that they must use in prayer.

ROMEO

O, then, dear saint, let lips do what hands do;
They pray, grant thou, lest faith turn to despair.

JULIET

Saints do not move, though grant for prayers' sake.

ROMEO

Then move not, while my prayer's effect I take.
Thus from my lips, by yours, my sin is purged.

JULIET

Then have my lips the sin that they have took.

ROMEO

Sin from thy lips? O trespass sweetly urged!
Give me my sin again.

JULIET

You kiss by th' book.

Starting with this conversation, explore how Shakespeare presents love in *Romeo and Juliet*.

Write about:
- how Shakespeare presents love in this extract
- how far Shakespeare presents love in the play as a whole.

[30 + 4 marks]

Your answer may include:

AO1 — show understanding of the text
- This extract reinforces Romeo and Juliet's romantic love for each other, but the kiss that they share also hints at their sexual desire.
- Throughout the play, the couple's love is passionate and intense. They put themselves at risk to be together, and they ultimately choose to die than live without each other.
- Prior to this extract, Romeo is lovesick because of his unrequited love for Rosaline. Shakespeare shows how unrequited love makes Romeo miserable. This contrasts with his reciprocated love with Juliet which makes him happy.
- Characters such as the Nurse and Mercutio use sexual language to remind the audience of sexual love. This contrasts with Romeo and Juliet's romantic love, making it seem innocent and pure in comparison.

AO2 — show understanding of the writer's language choices
- This is the couple's first meeting, so Shakespeare must make their love believable so that the audience understands why the couple risk so much to be together later in the play.
- Romeo and Juliet share a sonnet in their first exchange. Sonnets were traditionally a form of love poetry, so this reinforces the couple's romantic love.
- They finish each other's rhymes, which shows their instant connection.
- The religious language in this extract (e.g. "pilgrim", "saint", "pray") shows how pure and powerful their love is. However, later in the play the couple use dark imagery too. This reminds the audience that the couple are fated to die.

AO3 — relate the play to the context
- Romeo and Juliet kiss on their first meeting. This would have been quite scandalous to Elizabethan audiences, but it shows how the couple cannot resist each other, and how powerful their feelings are.
- Juliet's parents want her to marry Paris, and, as their only daughter, she would be expected to obey their wishes. Her arranged marriage would have been usual for noble women at the time, and a practical relationship that both families would benefit from.
- Shakespeare intertwines Romeo and Juliet's love with the theme of fate. They are fated to fall in love, but they are also fated to die.

This answer should be marked in accordance with the levels-based mark scheme on page 61.

Make sure your answer to this question is in paragraphs and full sentences. Bullet points have been used in this example answer to suggest some information you could include, but these suggestions are not exhaustive. There are four marks available for spelling, punctuation and grammar, so make sure you read through your answer carefully, correcting any mistakes.

THEMES: FATE AND FREE WILL

Romeo and Juliet are described in the Prologue as *"star-crossed"* (doomed). The idea their destinies are controlled by fate reoccurs throughout the play.

Fate

Fate is the idea that all events are pre-determined, and whatever you do, you cannot change fate's course. Although some people today still believe in fate and destiny, it was much more widely believed in Elizabethan times. Fate was closely associated with the stars and the heavens.

Throughout the play, Shakespeare makes multiple references to the idea of fate:

> These are just some examples. There are plenty more throughout the play.

Prologue

The Prologue summarises what will happen in the play before it has even begun. This introduces the idea of fate, and makes the audience feel helpless, as though nothing can be done to stop Romeo and Juliet from dying.

Comment: The Prologue would have been recited by the Chorus (a group of actors). Having several people chanting the Prologue in unison would have added to the eerie inevitability of the play's events.

Act 3

After he kills Tybalt in Act 3, Scene 1, Romeo calls himself *"fortune's fool"*. Romeo believes that fate (*"fortune"*) has made him act foolishly.

Act 5

Act 5, Scene 3 is the final scene of the play, and it reinforces the idea that Romeo and Juliet's destinies are controlled by fate. Romeo thinks that killing himself will *"shake the yoke of inauspicious stars"* (remove the control that fate has on his life). Ironically, the audience know that Romeo is fated to die, so his actions fulfil his destiny.

> Shakespeare also frequently uses **foreshadowing** throughout the play. Hinting at events that are yet to come makes them seem like fate when they happen.

Comment: Shakespeare suggests that you can't alter the course of fate.

The play ends just as the Prologue said it would, with Romeo and Juliet dying. This emphasises how fate is inescapable and inevitable.

Comment: Although the audience knew Romeo and Juliet were destined to die, their deaths would still be upsetting. This would provoke catharsis, the purging of emotion.

After the bodies of Romeo and Juliet are discovered, the Prince says: *"See what a scourge is laid upon your hate, / That heaven finds means to kill your joys with love"*. The Prince implies that fate (*"heaven"*) killed Romeo and Juliet as a punishment for their families' feud.

Free will

Free will is the opposite of fate. It is the idea that people have the power to choose their own destiny.

Shakespeare could be suggesting that Romeo and Juliet might have lived if they hadn't behaved so impulsively and irresponsibly.

- If the couple had told their parents the truth about their relationship, they might have avoided a lot of heartbreak.
- If Romeo hadn't killed Tybalt, he wouldn't have been banished, and the couple wouldn't have resorted to such drastic actions in Acts 4 and 5.
- If Romeo had visited the Friar before going to the Capulets' crypt in Act 5, he would have discovered that Juliet was still alive.

Shakespeare could also be suggesting that other people's actions affected the couple:

- If the Friar hadn't agreed to marry the couple, Romeo and Juliet might have taken things more slowly and been less impulsive.
- If the Capulets and Montagues cared more about their children than the feud, the couple might not have kept their love a secret.
- If Lord Capulet hadn't forced Juliet to marry Paris, she might have just waited for Romeo to return from exile.
- If Romeo had received the Friar's letter about Juliet's fake death, he wouldn't have killed himself.

> These are just a few examples of how the characters could have made different decisions which could have altered the course of the play.

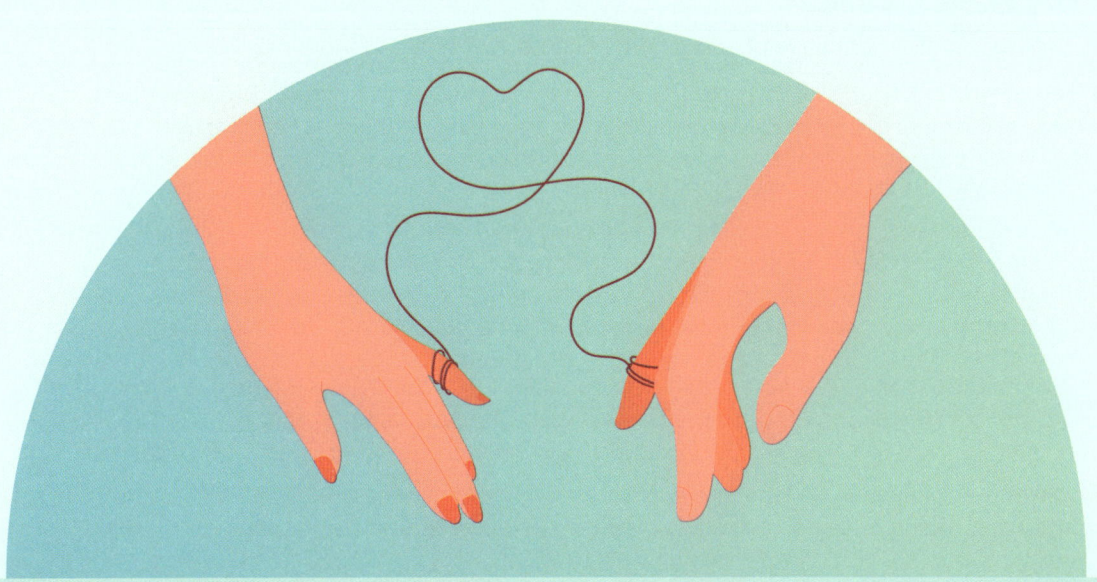

GCSE **English Literature | Romeo and Juliet**

THEMES: CONFLICT

The most obvious conflict within the play is the feud between the Montagues and the Capulets, but Shakespeare includes other types of conflict too.

The feud

It's never explained why the Capulets and Montagues hate each other. The feud is described as an *"ancient grudge"* implying that their hatred is so old, they've forgotten what started it.

> **Comment:** Not giving a reason for families' hatred of each other makes the feud seem even more pointless and irrational.

Shakespeare uses the feud for dramatic purposes:
- The feud proves the strength of Romeo and Juliet's love: they're prepared to defy their families' hatred to be together.
- Romeo and Juliet's love contrasts with the violence and hatred of the feud. This makes their relationship seem even more precious and romantic.
- The audience must believe that the feud is a genuine obstacle facing the couple. This makes their desperate actions seem plausible.
- The violence escalates throughout the play, and this increases the tension for the audience.
- The sword fights in Acts 1, 3 and 5 would have been exciting for audiences to watch.
- The play is a tragedy, so there must be some elements of conflict.

Impact of the feud

The feud and the importance of family honour cause conflict throughout the play.

The fight in Act 1, Scene 1 is instigated by the servants from the two families. The shows how the feud runs so deep that even the servants feel obliged to fight on their masters' behalf.

> **Comment:** The feud isn't just a petty grudge. It causes violence and bloodshed.

The brawl in Act 1, Scene 1 forces the Prince to introduce the death penalty to punish anyone caught fighting. This suggests that the feud is so bad that the Prince has to threaten the Capulets and Montagues with the most extreme form of punishment.

> **Comment:** Despite the severe nature of the punishment, it doesn't deter Mercutio, Tybalt and Romeo from fighting in Act 3, Scene 1. This presents the feud as unstoppable.

Tybalt is outraged when Romeo gate-crashes the party and he views it as an act of disrespect. This leads Tybalt to challenge Romeo to a duel so he can protect his family's honour.

> **Comment:** Romeo and Juliet meet for the first time at the Capulets' party. Tybalt's threat of violence shows how the feud hangs over the couple from the very first moment they meet.

Impact of the feud continued

In Act 3, Scene 1, Tybalt actively searches for Romeo and challenges him to a duel. When Romeo refuses to fight, Mercutio steps in to defend Romeo's honour.

Comment: Even though Romeo refuses to fight, he cannot stop the other characters from fighting. This shows the destructive and unstoppable nature of the feud.

The fight in Act 3, Scene 1 leads to the deaths of Mercutio and Tybalt, and Romeo being banished. The deaths of Mercutio and Tybalt only seem to worsen the feud.

Comment: Although the audience know from the Prologue that Romeo and Juliet are destined to die, the deaths of Mercutio and Tybalt would have been shocking.

Ultimately, the feud causes Romeo, Juliet, Lady Montague and Paris to die too.

Comment: None of the characters needed to die; their deaths could have been avoided. This shows how destructive and unnecessary the feud is.

At the end of the play, Montague and Capulet agree to end the feud. Shakespeare suggests that their hatred was so intense, that only the deaths of their children could end it.

Shakespeare presents the conflict as pointless.

Other types of conflict

A different type of conflict occurs in Act 3, Scene 5 between Juliet and her father when she refuses to marry Paris.

Comment: Capulet thinks that he has done his duty as a father by arranging a good match for his daughter. He thinks Juliet is being ungrateful as well as disobedient.

Capulet is furious and he:
- verbally abuses his daughter calling her a *"Disobedient wretch!"*.
- threatens to physically abuse her: *"My fingers itch"*.
- threatens to disown her: *"For, by my soul, I'll ne'er acknowledge thee"* and leave her to *"beg, starve, die in the streets"*.

Even though Juliet begs on her knees for her father to reconsider, Lord Capulet is unmoved by his daughter's pleas.

Comment: Juliet is torn between honouring her family's wishes and her own happiness.

Juliet begs on her knees to plead with Lord Capulet.

Read the following extract from Act 1, Scene 1. At this point in the play, Sampson and Gregory, two Capulet servants, have started a fight with some Montague servants in the streets of Verona.

SAMPSON
>Draw, if you be men. Gregory, remember thy swashing blow.

>*They fight*
>Enter **BENVOLIO**

BENVOLIO
>Part, fools!
>Put up your swords; you know not what you do.

>*Enter **TYBALT***

TYBALT
>What, art thou drawn among these heartless hinds?
>Turn thee, Benvolio, look upon thy death.

BENVOLIO
>I do but keep the peace: put up thy sword,
>Or manage it to part these men with me.

TYBALT
>What, drawn, and talk of peace! I hate the word,
>As I hate hell, all Montagues, and thee:
>Have at thee, coward!

>*They fight*
>*Enter, several of both houses, who join the fray; then enter Citizens, with clubs*

FIRST CITIZEN
>Clubs, bills, and partisans! strike! beat them down!
>Down with the Capulets! down with the Montagues!

>*Enter **CAPULET** in his gown, and **LADY CAPULET***

CAPULET
>What noise is this? Give me my long sword, ho!

Starting with this extract, explore how Shakespeare presents the effects of the conflict between the Capulet and Montague families.

Write about:
- how Shakespeare presents the effects of the conflict in this extract
- how Shakespeare presents the effects of the conflict in the play as whole.

[30 + 4 marks]

Your answer may include:

AO1 — show understanding of the text
- *In the extract, servants of the Montagues and Capulets are fighting. This shows how deep the feud runs: the servants are prepared to fight on behalf of their masters.*
- *Even when Benvolio tries to break up the fight, Tybalt forces Benvolio to duel. This shows how unstoppable the feud is, and how peace isn't an option.*
- *The reason for the families' hatred is never explained. This makes the feud seem pointless.*
- *The conflict causes the deaths of Mercutio, Tybalt, Lady Montague, Romeo and Juliet. It is only after Romeo and Juliet's death that the families agree to end the feud.*

AO2 — show understanding of the writer's language choices
- *This extract was taken from the very first scene of the play. This allows Shakespeare to establish the conflict as one of the most important elements of the play.*
- *Tybalt compares his hatred of Montagues to his hatred of hell. Since religion was so important in the 16th century, this emphasises just how strong his hatred is.*
- *During the extract, there would have been multiple actors on stage. This would have added to confused and intense atmosphere.*
- *Sword fights would have provided a dramatic spectacle for the audience.*
- *The citizen's line "Down with the Capulets! Down with the Montagues!" shows the negative impact the feud has on the people of Verona.*

AO3 — relate the play to the context
- *Conflict is linked to masculinity. Sampson says "Draw, if you be men", suggesting that peace was seen as a feminine attribute, and Tybalt calls Benvolio a "coward" for refusing to fight. This shows how masculinity contributes to the feud.*
- *Conflict is presented as futile and pointless, rather than honourable and necessary.*
- *The feud is used by Shakespeare as an obstacle that Romeo and Juliet must overcome to be together. This helps to prove the strength of their love.*
- *The conflict makes Romeo and Juliet's love seem more precious in comparison to the hatred caused by the feud.*

This answer should be marked in accordance with the levels-based mark scheme on page 61.

Make sure your answer to this question is in paragraphs and full sentences. Bullet points have been used in this example answer to suggest some information you could include, but these suggestions are not exhaustive. There are four marks available for spelling, punctuation and grammar, so make sure you read through your answer carefully, correcting any mistakes.

THEMES: GENDER

Some of Shakespeare's characters conform to gender stereotypes, while others rebel against them.

Femininity

Juliet

Sixteenth-century audiences would have expected Juliet to be submissive, obedient and chaste. However, once Juliet meets Romeo, she rebels against these conventions.
- She is assertive when she suggests that Romeo marry her.
- She disobeys her parents by refusing to marry Paris.
- She shows physical desire by kissing Romeo when they first meet.

As an unmarried noblewoman, Juliet's life is far more restricted than the other characters, for example, she cannot leave the house unaccompanied or without permission.

Comment: Most of Juliet's scenes take place indoors. This symbolises how she is restricted by her status and gender.

Masculinity

Romeo

Audiences would have also expected Romeo to display 'typical' male traits, such as being dominant and aggressive. However, Shakespeare subverts these stereotypes: Romeo is presented as peaceful and emotional.

Comment: Romeo's character contrasts with the hyper-masculine attitudes shown by other male characters in the play, such as Mercutio and Tybalt.

- He refuses to fight Tybalt and tries to break up the fight between Tybalt and Mercutio.
- He cries over Rosaline and uses romantic and poetic language to express his feelings.

Comment: Mercutio mocks Romeo for expressing 'unmasculine' behaviour, suggesting that Romeo's gentle nature was not seen as typical at the time.

Mercutio

Mercutio displays more 'typical' male behaviours. He focuses on sexual, rather than romantic, love, and he shows bravado when he provokes Tybalt into a sword fight.

Comment: This masculine aggression is presented as destructive: it escalates the feud since the male characters don't want to show weakness by backing down.

Despite this, Romeo is capable of aggression when he is provoked or overwhelmed. For example, when Mercutio is killed, Romeo is so blinded by revenge that he murders Tybalt.

EXAMINATION PRACTICE

> Read the following extract from Act 2, Scene 3.
> At this point in the play, Romeo has asked Friar Lawrence to marry him and Juliet.
>
> **ROMEO**
> Thou chid'st me oft for loving Rosaline.
>
> **FRIAR LAWRENCE**
> For doting, not for loving, pupil mine.
>
> **ROMEO**
> And bad'st me bury love.
>
> **FRIAR LAWRENCE**
> Not in a grave,
> To lay one in, another out to have.
>
> **ROMEO**
> I pray thee, chide not; she whom I love now
> Doth grace for grace and love for love allow;
> The other did not so.
>
> **FRIAR LAWRENCE**
> O, she knew well
> Thy love did read by rote and could not spell.
> But come, young waverer, come, go with me,
> In one respect I'll thy assistant be;
> For this alliance may so happy prove,
> To turn your households' rancour to pure love.
>
> **ROMEO**
> O, let us hence; I stand on sudden haste.
>
> **FRIAR LAWRENCE**
> Wisely and slow; they stumble that run fast.

Starting with this point in the play, explore how Shakespeare presents relationships between adults and young people in *Romeo and Juliet*.

Write about:
- how Shakespeare presents relationships between adults and young people in this conversation.
- how far Shakespeare presents relationships between adults and young people in the play as a whole.

[30 + 4 marks]

EXAMINATION PRACTICE ANSWERS

In *Romeo and Juliet*, Shakespeare presents relationships between parents and their children as distant, formal and, at times, hostile. This was not unusual in the 15th century, as noble children were often raised by nannies and servants, so parents didn't bond as closely with their children. Instead, both Romeo and Juliet have close relationships with maternal and paternal figures: the Nurse and Friar Lawrence. The Nurse was Juliet's wet nurse, and helped raise Juliet from childhood. As a result, the Nurse seems more of a mother-figure to Juliet than Lady Capulet. Romeo, on the other hand, has a close relationship with Friar Lawrence. Since religion was an important aspect of 15th-century society, clergymen offered spiritual and moral guidance to their congregation. The extract shows this close relationship between Friar Lawrence and Romeo.

Firstly, Romeo trusts the Friar with his secrets. Romeo has confided in the Friar about his infatuation with Rosaline (*"Thou chid'st me oft for loving Rosaline"*), whereas Romeo has kept his feelings for Rosaline secret from his parents. Similarly, Romeo tells the Friar about his love for Juliet, and asks the Friar to marry them. This shows the closeness between the Friar and Romeo, as Romeo does not confide in his parents or his friends about his love for Juliet. Shakespeare reinforces this close, trusting relationship in the dialogue between the characters. The Friar uses terms of endearment towards Romeo such as *"pupil mine"*, as well as sharing lines of iambic pentameter with Romeo. For example, *"And bad'st me bury love. / Not in a grave"*. Completing each other's lines reinforces the intimacy between the characters.

Similarly, elsewhere in the play, Juliet has a very close relationship with the Nurse. Juliet confides in the Nurse about her clandestine relationship with Romeo, and the Nurse acts as a go-between, delivering messages between the couple, and even arranging for Romeo to sneak into Juliet's bedroom so that they can consummate the marriage. The Nurse's involvement in the couple's relationship puts her job at risk, since she is betraying her employers, the Capulets. This shows that the Nurse is willing to disregard her job security to make sure that Juliet is happy.

Conversely, Shakespeare presents Juliet's relationship with her parents as formal and distant. Juliet's mother, Lady Capulet, wants Juliet to enter an arranged marriage with Paris, even though the couple have never met. Although arranged marriages were frequent for wealthy families in the 15th century, this suggests that Lady Capulet is more concerned with the status and wealth that the union could bring, rather than her daughter's happiness in marriage. Juliet also has a very tense relationship with her father. When Juliet declines to marry Paris in Act 3, Scene 5, her father is outraged that Juliet would disobey him. Society in the 15th century was patriarchal, and fathers expected complete obedience from their daughters. Capulet responds by verbally abusing his daughter and threatening to disown her, showing how little regard he has for Juliet's happiness and wellbeing.

In conclusion, Shakespeare presents a variety of relationships between adults and young people in the play. Romeo and Juliet have close relationships with those characters who are willing to help and support them, like the Nurse and Friar Lawrence, and have more distant relationships with those adults who disregard their happiness, such as their parents. This outlook on cross-generational relationships is still true today, which reinforces the universality of Shakespeare's plays to the modern audience.

LEVELS-BASED MARK SCHEMES FOR EXTENDED RESPONSE QUESTIONS

Questions that require extended writing use levels. The whole answer will be marked together to determine which level it fits into and which mark it should be awarded.

The descriptors have been written in simple language to give an indication of the expectations of each level. See the AQA website for the official mark schemes used.

Level	Students' answers tend to...
6 (26–30 marks)	- Focus on the text as conscious construct (i.e. a play written by Shakespeare intended to have a deliberate effect). - Produce a logical and well-structured response which closely uses the text to explore their argument / interpretation. - Analyse the writer's craft by considering the effects of a writer's choice, linked closely to meanings. - Understand the writer's purpose and context.
5 (21–25 marks)	- Start to think about ideas in a more developed way. - Think about the deeper meaning of a text and start to explore alternative interpretations. - Start to focus on specific elements of writer's craft, linked to meanings. - Focus more on abstract concepts, such as themes and ideas, than narrative events or character feelings.
4 (16–20 marks)	- Sustain a focus on an idea, or a particular technique. - Start to consider how the text works and what the writer is doing. - Use examples effectively to support their points. - Explain the effect of a writer's method on the text, with a clear focus on it having been consciously written. - Show an understanding of ideas and themes.
3 (11–15 marks)	- Explain their ideas. - Demonstrate knowledge of the text as a whole. - Show awareness of the concept of themes. - Identify the effects of a range of methods on reader.
2 (6–10 marks)	- Support their comments by using references to / from the text. - Make comments that are generally relevant to the question. - Identify at least one method and possibly make some comment on the effect of it on the reader.
1 (1–5 marks)	- Describe the text. - Retell the narrative. - Make references to, rather than use references from, the text.
0 marks	Nothing worthy of credit / nothing written.

INDEX

A
acts 6
antagonist 2
antithesis 11, 31
apostrophes 7
apothecary 28
arranged marriage 3, 13, 23, 36
aside 6

B
Balthasar 28–30
Benvolio 12, 13, 15, 16, 18, 20, 21, 45
bigamy 4

C
catharsis 2, 52
Catholicism 4
Chorus 12, 52
City Watch 29, 30
comic relief 42, 43
confession 4
conflict 12, 54, 55
consummate (a marriage) 4
context 3–5

D
dramatic irony 6, 11, 15, 21, 23, 24, 28, 29

F
fatal flaw 2, 15
fate 11, 12, 21, 28, 30, 33, 52, 53
femininity 58
feud 12, 18, 20, 21, 22, 30, 54, 55
foil 11, 15
foreshadowing 11, 13, 18, 20, 21, 23, 28, 37, 52
free will 52, 53
Friar John 29
Friar Lawrence 17–19, 22, 25–27, 29, 30, 41

G
gender 58
Gregory 12

I
iambic pentameter 8, 9
imagery 11, 15, 49
Italy 3

J
Juliet 2, 13, 14, 16, 17, 19, 21–27, 29, 30, 36–38, 48

L
Lady Capulet 13, 14, 21, 23, 24, 27, 30, 46
Lady Montague 13, 21, 47
Lord Capulet 13, 15, 21, 23, 24, 26, 27, 30, 46
Lord Montague 13, 21, 30, 47
love 13, 48
  doomed love 37, 49
  romantic love 49
  sexual love 11, 32, 37, 49
  unrequited love 13, 31, 48

M
Mantua 22, 25, 28
masculinity 58
masked ball 13, 15
Mercutio 15, 16, 18, 20, 42, 49
metaphor 11, 16, 21
monologue 9, 22, 43
musicians 27

N
Nurse 14, 17–19, 21– 24, 26, 27, 43

O
oxymorons 11, 13, 22, 31, 37

P
pace 28
Paris 13, 14, 23, 27, 29, 44, 49
patriarchal society 3, 23, 46
personification 11
Peter 13, 27
poison 11, 25, 26, 28

Prince 13, 21, 30, 45
Prologue 9, 12, 16, 28
pronouns 7
prose 9, 14, 43
protagonist 2
puns 11, 14, 20

R
religion 4
repetition 27
rhyming couplets 9
rhythm 8
Romeo 2, 13, 15–23, 28–33, 48
Rosaline 13, 15, 16, 18, 31, 48

S
Sampson 12
scenes 6
sentence order 8
setting 3
Shakespeare's Globe Theatre 6
Shakespeare, William 2
shared lines 8
simile 11
soliloquy 9, 10, 16, 17, 21, 26, 28, 37, 38
sonnet 2, 9, 12, 15, 16, 49
stage directions 6
suicide 4, 21, 25, 33
syllables 8
symbolism 10

T
Ten Commandments 24
tension 11, 19, 20, 23, 28, 29
theatre 5
tragedy 2, 12
Tybalt 12, 15, 18, 20, 21, 44

V
verbs 7
Verona 3, 12
verse 8

W
wet nurse 14

NOTES, DOODLES AND EXAM DATES

Doodles

Key dates

Paper 1:

Paper 2:

ACKNOWLEDGMENTS

The questions in the ClearRevise textbook are the sole responsibility of the authors and have neither been provided nor approved by the examination board.

Every effort has been made to trace and acknowledge ownership of copyright. The publishers will be happy to make any future amendments with copyright owners that it has not been possible to contact. The publisher would like to thank the following companies and individuals who granted permission for the use of their images in this textbook.

Page 2 — William Shakespeare © Nicku / Shutterstock.com
Page 4 — © Donald Cooper / Photostage
Page 5 — Globe Theatre © Nick Brundle Photography / Shutterstock.com
Page 6 — Globe Theatre © RichartPhotos / Shutterstock.com
Page 8 — © Donald Cooper / Photostage
Page 9 — © Donald Cooper / Photostage
Page 12 — Romeo and Juliet © Relativity Media / Everett Collection / Alamy Stock Photo
Page 14 — © Donald Cooper / Photostage
Page 15 — Relativity Media's 'Romeo and Juliet' © PictureLux / The Hollywood Archive / Alamay Stock Photo
Page 17 — © Donald Cooper / Photostage
Page 17 — © Donald Cooper / Photostage
Page 19 — © Donald Cooper / Photostage
Page 20 — © Donald Cooper / Photostage
Page 22 — © Donald Cooper / Photostage
Page 24 — © Donald Cooper / Photostage
Page 25 — © Donald Cooper / Photostage
Page 26 — © Donald Cooper / Photostage
Page 28 — © Donald Cooper / Photostage
Page 30 — © Donald Cooper / Photostage
Page 31 — © Donald Cooper / Photostage
Page 32 — © Donald Cooper / Photostage
Page 33 — © Donald Cooper / Photostage
Page 36 — © Donald Cooper / Photostage
Page 37 — © Donald Cooper / Photostage
Page 38 — © Donald Cooper / Photostage
Page 41 — © Donald Cooper / Photostage
Page 42 — © Donald Cooper / Photostage
Page 43 — © Donald Cooper / Photostage
Page 44 — © Donald Cooper / Photostage
Page 45 — © Donald Cooper / Photostage
Page 46 — © Donald Cooper / Photostage
Page 47 — © Donald Cooper / Photostage
Page 48 — © Donald Cooper / Photostage
Page 55 — © Donald Cooper / Photostage
Page 55 — © Donald Cooper / Photostage

All other photographs and graphics © Shutterstock.

EXAMINATION TIPS

With your examination practice, use a boundary approximation using the following table. Be aware that the grade boundaries can vary from year to year, so they should be used as a guide only.

Grade	9	8	7	6	5	4	3	2	1
Boundary	88%	79%	71%	61%	52%	43%	31%	21%	10%

1. Read the question carefully. Don't give an answer to a question that you think is appearing (or wish was appearing!) rather than the actual question.
2. Spend time reading through the extract, and think about what happens before and after, and how it links to other parts of the play. The statement above the extract will help you identify where in the play it is from.
3. It's worth jotting down a quick plan to make sure your answer includes sufficient detail and is focused on the question.
4. The question will ask you about the extract and the play as a whole, but you don't need to spend an equal amount of time on both. If you're struggling to make close textual references about the extract, you can concentrate on the rest of the play instead.
5. A discussion of Shakespeare's methods can include his language choices, but also structural choices (such as the ordering of events), how characters develop, and what their actions tell you about their characterisation.
6. Include details from the text to support your answer. These details might be quotes, or they can be references to the text. Don't worry if you can't remember quotes from other parts of the play. You will be marked on the strength of your answer to the question, not the accuracy of your quotations.
7. Make sure your handwriting is legible. The examiner can't award you marks if they can't read what you've written.
8. The examiner will be impressed if you can correctly use technical terms like 'foil', 'soliloquy', 'iambic pentameter', 'rhyming couplets' but to be awarded the best marks, you need to explore the effect of these techniques.
9. Use linking words and phrases to show you are developing your points or comparing information, for example, "this reinforces", "this shows that" and "on the other hand". This helps to give your answer structure, and makes it easier for the examiner to award you marks.
10. If you need extra paper, make sure you clearly signal that your answer is continued elsewhere. Remember that longer answers don't necessarily score more highly than shorter, more concise answers.
11. There are 4 marks available for spelling, punctuation and grammar. Save some time at the end of the exam to read through your answer and correct any mistakes.

Good luck!

New titles coming soon!

Revision, re-imagined

These guides are everything you need to ace your exams and beam with pride. Each topic is laid out in a beautifully illustrated format that is clear, approachable and as concise and simple as possible.

They have been expertly compiled and edited by subject specialists, highly experienced examiners, industry professionals and a good dollop of scientific research into what makes revision most effective. Past examination questions are essential to good preparation, improving understanding and confidence.

- Hundreds of marks worth of examination style questions
- Answers provided for all questions within the books
- Illustrated topics to improve memory and recall
- Specification references for every topic
- Examination tips and techniques
- Free Python solutions pack (CS Only)

Absolute clarity is the aim.

Explore the series and add to your collection at **www.clearrevise.com**

Available from all good book shops

  @pgonlinepub

ClearRevise — Illustrated revision and practice
AQA GCSE **Physical Education** 8582

ClearRevise — Illustrated revision and practice
OCR **Creative iMedia** Levels 1/2 J834 (R093, R094)

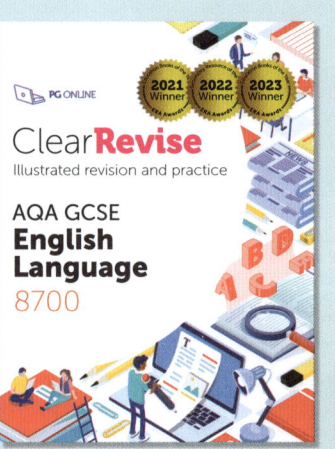

ClearRevise — Illustrated revision and practice
AQA GCSE **English Language** 8700

ClearRevise — Illustrated revision and practice
Edexcel GCSE **History** 1HI0
Weimar and Nazi Germany, 1918–39
Paper 3

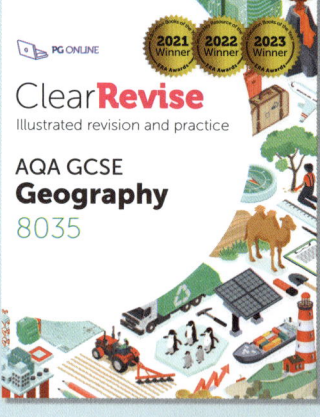

ClearRevise — Illustrated revision and practice
AQA GCSE **Geography** 8035

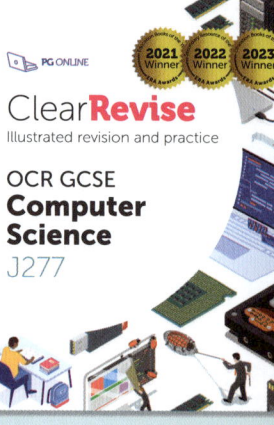

ClearRevise — Illustrated revision and practice
OCR GCSE **Computer Science** J277

ClearRevise — Illustrated revision and practice
AQA GCSE English Literature **An Inspector Calls** By J. B. Priestley 8702

ClearRevise — Illustrated revision and practice
Edexcel GCSE **Business** 1BS0

ClearRevise — Illustrated revision and practice
AQA GCSE **Combined Science** Trilogy 8464 Foundation & Higher

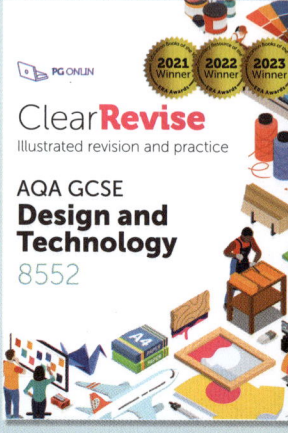

ClearRevise — Illustrated revision and practice
AQA GCSE **Design and Technology** 8552